THE GASTROPARESIS COOKBOOK

THE GASTROPARESIS COOKBOOK

102
DELICIOUS, NUTRITIOUS RECIPES FOR GASTROPARESIS RELIEF

Karen Frazier

ROCKRIDGE
PRESS

For my family

Front cover photo: Linda Pugliese/Stockfood. Back cover photos, from left: Sam Stowell/Stockfood; Samantha Linsell/Stockfood; Michael Boyny/Stockfood.

Interior Photos: Liv Friis/Stockfood, pg. 2; Linda Pugliese/Stockfood, pg. 6; PhotoCuisine/Thys/Supperdelux/Stockfood, pg. 8; Ewgenija Schall/Stockfood, pg. 14; Oxana Afanasieva/Stockfood, pg. 24; Magdalena Paluchowska/Stockfood, pg. 36; Gräfe & Unzer Verlag/mona binner PHOTOGRAPHIE/Stockfood, pg. 52; PhotoCuisine/Thys/Supperdelux/Stockfood, pg. 66; Samantha Linsell/Stockfood, pg. 78; Sam Stowell/Stockfood, pg. 90; Michael Boyny/Stockfood, pg. 108; Jalag / Julia Hoersch/Stockfood, pg. 124; Rua Castilho/Stockfood, pg. 140. All other photos Shutterstock.com.

Illustrations on pg. 18 © Tom Bingham.

ISBN: Print 978-1-62315-698-5 | eBook 978-1-62315-699-2

5 TIPS FOR EASING GASTROPARESIS SYMPTOMS THROUGH DIET

While diet alone cannot cure gastroparesis, carefully managing what you eat can help control your symptoms. When managing your gastroparesis via diet, consider the following strategies:

1 **Avoid excessive intake of high-fiber foods.** Foods very high in fiber, such as legumes, whole grains, and raw, unpeeled vegetables and fruits, can all cause delayed stomach emptying. To include vegetables and fruits in your diet, peel and cook them first, or substitute fruit or vegetable juice.

2 **Minimize fat intake.** Keep fat intake to less than 40 grams of fat per day and avoid eating a lot of fat in any given meal. Fat can delay stomach emptying, so it's important to limit your consumption. Small amounts of healthy fats, such as avocado or coconut milk, can help increase your calorie count without causing a flare-up, but it is highly individual, so you need to monitor these ingredients to determine how they affect you.

3 **During symptom outbreaks, switch to a liquid diet.** When you are very symptomatic, consume a liquid diet until symptoms subside. Use nutrient- and calorie-dense liquids, such as vegetable and meat broths, fruit or vegetable juices, and other forms of liquid nutrition.

4 **Keep portion sizes small.** Eating large meals can also delay stomach emptying and cause symptoms to flare. Instead of eating three large meals, try to eat five to six small meals throughout the day.

5 **Drink liquids separately from meals.** While many people like to wash down meals and snacks with a beverage, it's best to have your beverages between meals so your stomach can empty more quickly. Have small sips of water with a meal, but drink your main beverages 30 minutes before or 60 minutes after you eat.

CONTENTS

FOREWORD

Colleen Beener

G-PACT OPERATIONS DIRECTOR

So, you've been diagnosed with gastroparesis and are wondering—what in the world can I eat? You're not alone! Every gastroparesis patient has to navigate through the maze of finding what foods to eat that are nourishing and healthy, yet also manage to keep from hugging the porcelain throne or popping Zofran like they are candy. It is not an easy maze to navigate.

I know exactly how you feel. I was diagnosed with gastroparesis in 2001, after three years of searching for the reason why my stomach was rejecting everything I put into it. Back then, there were very few resources for help, and no diet plans available. Everything was trial and error, and I tried to heal my stomach by eating healthy foods that I would later come to find were the worst things I could eat. No wonder I was so sick!

According to the most recent statistics, 1 in 25 people suffer from gastroparesis. What used to be considered a rare disease is now affecting 4 percent of the population. We don't know if gastroparesis is more prevalent, or if doctors have become more adept at making the diagnosis. But we do know that there are a lot of us suffering from this disease!

Being so ill makes us desperate to find that magic pill or potion that will make things better. Unfortunately, there currently is no magic that will help gastroparesis patients. We have to plod along, figuring it all out as we go along. Over the past few years, more resources became available, including a few cookbooks. But, as patients, we still want more. This cookbook is one of the new resources available to us.

Karen Frazier is skilled in putting together cookbooks that cater to individuals with different health issues that affect their ability to eat nutritiously. In this cookbook for gastroparesis patients, Karen worked hard to incorporate healthy foods into recipes that fall within acceptable guidelines for gastroparesis sufferers. She understands our issues and has come up with pleasing flavors and textures that are gentle on our tummies.

In addition, even though we may be ill, many of us still cook for our families. Making a different meal for the family is time consuming and exhausting. But in this cookbook there are recipes that you can prepare for everyone. And they're healthy recipes that are also tasty, so your family should love them. Plus, many can be prepared in a slow cooker, saving yourself from wasting precious energy cooking over a hot stove. Karen also gives hints on preparing things in bulk, which cuts down on prep time and effort.

One thing that I've found while volunteering with G-PACT is that there is no single diet that will work for everyone. Medical professionals will tell us to eat six small meals that are low in fat and fiber. And while that works for some, it does not work for us all. So check out the recipes here and find those that look enticing. You can always tweak things a little or purée some of the dishes to make them amenable to your digestive system. While the things in this cookbook will not work for all, there is a good cross-section of recipes that should work for many.

If you need other support options, check out our website at www.g-pact.org. You can also find us on Facebook and Twitter. Just search for G-PACT and a number of groups will appear—we have something for everyone. Back when I was first diagnosed, G-PACT was just an idea in the minds of a few gastroparesis patients. I was lucky to find them shortly after they were formed in 2001 and credit G-PACT and their group members with addressing my fears and helping me find the best treatment options for me. I have been a volunteer with them for about 13 years and see firsthand how many people need support. We would be honored to have you join us!

Enjoy the recipes in this cookbook. Just because we cannot eat like normal people, that doesn't mean that we can't have interesting, tasty, healthy food.

INTRODUCTION

For people with gastric motility disorders, such as gastroparesis, it may feel as if it's impossible to live a normal life. So much in our culture revolves around food, and when you're severely limited in what and how much you can eat due to a gastrointestinal disorder, it can make interactions with food seem daunting.

Although I don't have gastroparesis, I understand this feeling well. I have lived for most of my life with another disorder, celiac disease, which when undiagnosed and untreated can cause severe gastrointestinal symptoms, along with nutrient malabsorption and malnutrition. I remained undiagnosed for the better part of two decades and suffered from severe gastrointestinal symptoms, chronic severe GERD, malnutrition, and anemia. Eating felt like a game of Russian roulette, because I never knew when I'd wind up with severe symptoms shortly after a meal. Over the course of 20 years, I underwent multiple medical tests trying to ascertain the cause of my severe food-related symptoms, and even had doctors who suggested my symptoms were psychosomatic in nature. An accurate diagnosis and changing how I eat has allowed me to better manage my symptoms.

With gastroparesis and other gastrointestinal disorders like undiagnosed celiac disease, just the thought of eating can become fraught with worry. You never know if a meal, trip to a restaurant, or family gathering is going to leave you out of commission for the next few hours, the next few days, or even the next few weeks.

Unfortunately, you can't just stop eating food. Instead, it's important to identify a way of eating that helps minimize symptoms and flare-ups, allowing you to meet your body's nutritional requirements while still living your life in the best way possible. While the thought of totally overhauling your diet and restricting or eliminating a large number of foods may seem overwhelming, the resulting management of symptoms and improved quality of life makes the effort worthwhile.

This book strives to make that transition as simple as possible for you. The chapters that follow clearly outline the types of foods you can eat and their manner of preparation in order for you to gain better control of your condition, and also provide easy-to-follow recipes for delicious foods.

Every person's body is unique and different, but there are some general guidelines that can help people with gastroparesis manage their symptoms. However, as is often the case with gastrointestinal diagnoses, gastroparesis doesn't exist in a vacuum. It often occurs in conjunction with other conditions that have special dietary requirements, such as diabetes, endocrine disorders, GERD, and autoimmune disorders. The recipes in this book are labeled to show how each fits in with other specific diets such as gluten-free, GERD-friendly, low-FODMAP, and SIBO-friendly diets. Recipes also include tips on how to alter them to fit within certain specialized diets, giving you the ability to further customize the foods you eat on this plan for more effective symptom management.

This book also provides information and tips from other people suffering from gastroparesis. Their experiences can help you learn how to adapt your eating and lifestyle in ways that allow you to live as well as you possibly can with gastroparesis.

Support groups can help, as well (see page 193 in Resources). These groups offer encouragement and understanding from others who are dealing with the same issues you have, as well as helpful information and recipes. The nonprofit organization Gastroparesis Patient Association for Cures and Treatment (G-PACT), which began in 2001, is a strong community of support and offers services for people who suffer from gastroparesis and other types of digestive tract paralysis.

Of course, as with many medical conditions, diet is just one piece of the puzzle. While you may be better able to manage your symptoms following the eating plan and using the recipes in this book, it's important that you continue to work with your health-care provider on lifestyle and medical management of your gastroparesis in order to support your body's unique needs. The information in this book is not intended to replace the advice and care of your medical health professionals.

All of the foods and recipes in this book are designed to provide you with as much nutrition as possible. The recipes minimize processed, expensive, or hard-to-find ingredients, providing you with easy-to-prepare dishes made from whole, healthy foods. These recipes are designed to help you improve your diet, allowing you to live a fulfilling life with gastroparesis. While it may take a little bit of effort to change the types of foods you eat, the results are well worth your time and energy.

PART ONE

The Basics of Eating Well with Gastroparesis

1

HOW GASTROPARESIS AFFECTS YOU

If you've learned you have gastroparesis, chances are you've been chasing an accurate diagnosis for a while, mostly because it can take time for your health-care professional to correctly determine which gastrointestinal disorder is causing your symptoms. While your gastroparesis diagnosis may be a bit scary, knowing what you are dealing with allows you to make lifestyle changes that will help you make empowered choices about your health.

A Misunderstood Problem

Articles appearing in *Neurogastroenterology Motility* (2006) and the *Medscape Journal* (2008) cite an estimated 4 percent of the population in the United States suffer from some degree of delayed gastric emptying. GastroparesisClinic.org notes that exact statistics are difficult to track. This is in great part because not only does gastroparesis have numerous symptoms but also these symptoms are similar to other functional gastrointestinal disorders. This overlap often results in different diagnostic interpretations from health-care professionals. Another contributing factor to the problem of inexact numbers is that gastroparesis is not yet widely recognized or understood in the medical field. One statistic of note, however, is that women are more commonly affected with gastroparesis than men—about 80 percent of all people with gastroparesis are women. Gastroparesis is a serious issue, and receiving appropriate treatment is essential. The delay in gastric emptying can cause a number of complications, including malnutrition or under nutrition, and weight loss. If gastroparesis causes you to eat very little or your body to not receive and absorb the nutrients in the foods, then deficiencies in such nutrients as iron (anemia), vitamin B_{12}, calcium, magnesium, and potassium can result. All of these deficiencies increase the risk of other diseases and illnesses.

Likewise, patients experiencing other gastrointestinal symptoms such as nausea and vomiting may become severely dehydrated and experience electrolyte deficiencies. Seeking medical treatment and lifestyle modifications are critical to supporting your health. According to the March 2015 article in the medical journal *Gastroenterology Clinics of North America*, hospitalizations from gastroparesis started rising in 1995, with an even greater rise in the rate after 2000. Pharmaceutical companies, recognizing the growing numbers of patients, are running clinical trials throughout the country to test new drugs for effectiveness as well as for side effects.

As medical organizations and institutions such as the Mayo Clinic continue to conduct studies, trials, and research on how to improve diagnosis, management, and treatment of the condition, better information about the causes and frequency of gastroparesis should also improve.

Possible Causes and Coexisting Conditions

The American College of Gastroenterology notes that gastroparesis has many causes, as it is often secondary to other conditions. Those included in this section are only a partial list and appear in order of what is generally thought to be the most to least common.

Causes of gastroparesis include:

- Diabetes (type 1 and type 2)
- Idiopathic
- Infections
- Abdominal surgery

- Anorexia and bulimia
- Endocrine disorders, such as hypothyroidism
- Autoimmune disorders, such as lupus or scleroderma
- Certain medications

With so many causes of gastroparesis, different diets may be required to help manage certain conditions, such as diabetes. To that end, many of the recipes offer substitutions to help you manage these conditions with diet.

DIABETES

Gastroparesis tends to occur more often in people with type 1 diabetes than in people with type 2 diabetes, and GastroparesisClinic .org estimates that 20 to 50 percent of people with long-term diabetes have gastroparesis. According to the American Diabetes Association (ADA), a common complication of poorly controlled diabetes is neuropathy, or damage to the nerves. This may include the vagus nerve, which controls contractions of gastric muscles in the stomach. Damage to this nerve can result in gastroparesis. The ADA notes that the best way minimize this nerve damage is by controlling blood sugar, via diet or medications such as insulin.

IDIOPATHIC

Idiopathic means the cause is unknown. What *is* currently known is that idiopathic gastroparesis can occur following an infection, but does not occur due to the presence of another condition. Not understanding how you developed gastroparesis can be very frustrating. Though Johns Hopkins Medicine reports a

third of people with the condition have no identifiable cause, 30 to 50 percent of these people do have a history of previous viral illness.

INFECTIONS

When gastroparesis occurs after an infection, the condition is considered to be idiopathic (arising spontaneously or from unknown causes). The National Organization for Rare Disorders reports that a hospital providing tertiary care (health care from specialists) found that 36 percent of their 146 patients with gastroparesis cases were idiopathic.

Common Symptoms

Following are the most common symptoms of gastroparesis according to the American College of Gastroenterology. People with severe or ongoing symptoms should seek medical care in order to obtain accurate diagnosis and effective treatment.

- Bloating or stomach distention
- Colicky abdominal pain
- Difficulty controlling blood sugar
- Early fullness when eating (feeling full after just a few bites)
- Frequent or persistent GERD (gastro-esophageal reflux disease, or heartburn) that may not respond to medications
- Nausea and vomiting
- Nutrient deficiencies
- Weight loss

How Gastroparesis Works

Gastroparesis occurs when your stomach delays emptying due to poorly functioning or nonfunctioning muscles.

In a healthy digestive system, after being chewed and swallowed your food moves through your alimentary canal and into your stomach via muscle contractions. When the food reaches your stomach, a sphincter (the pyloric sphincter) at the bottom of the stomach closes off access to the small intestines so that further digestion can occur. With the food and digestive fluids held in the stomach by the closed pyloric sphincter, the vagus nerve causes the gastric muscles in the walls of the stomach to contract, churning the digestive fluids with the food, liquefying it further so that nutrients can be easily extracted when the food reaches the small intestines. Once digestion in the stomach is complete, contractions of gastric muscles push open the pyloric sphincter, and food enters the intestines where nutrient absorption begins.

In people with gastroparesis, however, the gastric muscles contract poorly or not at all due to an improperly functioning vagus nerve. Food then moves slowly from the stomach or not at all. Due to the lack of churning in the stomach, the food that moves into the small intestine may be poorly digested, which makes it more difficult for your body to absorb nutrients.

The images at the right will better show you how gastroparesis affects your digestive processes.

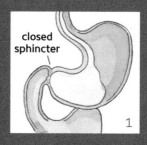

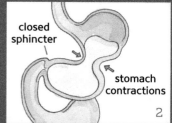

1 In a healthy digestive system, as food and fluids flow into your stomach through your alimentary canal, the pyloric sphincter closes and holds the food in place so that the stomach's digestive processes can occur without undigested foods escaping into the small intestine.

2 Once the food and fluids reach the stomach, the vagus nerve causes the gastric muscles of the stomach to contract and relax, churning the partially digested food and grinding it into smaller pieces while mixing it with gastric juices and turning it into a substance called chyme.

3 In a healthy digestive system, once the chyme has reached the appropriate state, gastric muscle churning opens the pyloric sphincter so it can move into the small intestines for nutrient absorption.

4 In a person with gastroparesis, the vagus nerve doesn't cause adequate churning (or it may not cause churning at all), which inhibits food from breaking down into chyme and prevents or delays the opening of the pyloric sphincter.

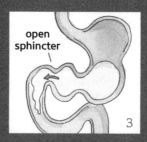

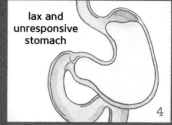

GastroparesisClinic.org offers a similar percent of gastroparesis cases as idiopathic. The infections that preceded the condition may vary, but include an array of gut illnesses, such as food poisoning, Norwalk virus, parasitic infections, mononucleosis (mono), and the herpes virus among others. A common link between these and other patient-reported illnesses may be inflammation, part of the body's immune response to illness. This inflammation can lead to damage of the vagus nerve, which results in gastroparesis.

ABDOMINAL SURGERY

Abdominal surgery can cause damage to the vagus nerve. Inflammation or infection arising as a result of abdominal surgery may also damage the vagus nerve. Many types of upper abdominal surgery are associated with gastroparesis, and may include:

- Bariatric surgery
- Fundoplication surgery for GERD
- Heart or lung transplants
- Peptic ulcer surgery

A 2007 article in the journal *Current Gastroenterology Reports* notes that post-surgical gastroparesis may resolve with time as the vagus nerve heals or the nervous system adapts to the nerve damage. In some cases, though, the condition may be permanent; if for example, the vagus nerve is severed, it will not grow back. The journal article suggests that electrical stimulation shows promise as a treatment of post-surgical gastroparesis. However, UW Health of the University of Wisconsin–Madison reports that in many

cases a gastric neurostimulator has not been found to improve stomach emptying. That being said, it can improve symptoms of gastroparesis and therefore improve nutrition in patients, but with varying levels of results.

ANOREXIA AND BULIMIA

People with eating disorders may also experience gastroparesis. This most likely occurs due to the abnormal stomach function required of these disorders. In the case of anorexia, it may arise from disuse of the stomach muscles and nerves, while with bulimia it may result from overuse. The American College of Gastroenter-ology notes that in most people who have gastroparesis associated with an eating disorder symptoms improve when eating habits normalize.

ENDOCRINE DISORDERS

For people with endocrine (hormonal) disorders such as Addison's disease, hyperparathyroidism, or hypothyroidism, imbalances in hormones may influence gastric nerve or motor function, according to excerpts from a 2010 meeting of the American Gastroenterological Association and the American Neurogastroenterology and Motility Society. This can affect hormones associated with hunger and satiation, among other functions. Careful management of hormonal issues can help improve gastroparesis symptoms.

AUTOIMMUNE DISORDERS

There appears to be a correlation between autoimmune disease (such as multiple sclerosis and Parkinson's disease) and autoinflammatory disorders (such as scleroderma) and gastroparesis. According to Womenshealth.gov, one of the key markers of both autoimmune and autoinflammatory disease is inflammation, which may cause damage to the vagus nerve, possibly resulting in gastroparesis. Controlling inflammation is key in this case, so doctors may recommend anti-inflammatory treatments and lifestyle changes.

MEDICATIONS

Some medications are associated with delayed gastric emptying. According to the American College of Gastroenterology, the most common medications associated with delayed stomach emptying include:

- Calcium channel blockers, such as amlodipine, felodipine, or verapamil
- Clonidine
- Dopamine agonists, such as ropinirole or pramipexole
- Lithium
- Narcotics, such as hydrocodone, oxycodone, or codeine
- Nicotine
- Progesterone
- Tricyclic antidepressants (TCAs), such as amitriptyline (Elavil), doxepin (Sinequan or Deptran), or protriptyline

In general, discontinuing medications that cause delayed gastric emptying will normalize gastric function.

OTHER CORRELATIONS

Some studies, such as one published in a January 2010 issue of the *Journal of Clinical Gastroenterology*, suggest there is a correlation between SIBO (small intestine bacterial overgrowth) and gastroparesis. At this time, however, it is unknown what the link between the two is, just that one exists. A low-FODMAP diet, which is low in certain types of simple carbohydrates referred to as FODMAPs, may help improve SIBO. You can read more about this diet in the next chapter.

Spotlight on Diabetes and Gastroparesis

As previously noted, gastroparesis is common in people with poorly controlled diabetes. Johns Hopkins Medicine notes that 30 to 60 percent of people with diabetes (either type 1 or type 2) develop some form of autonomic neuropathy, and that gastroparesis is one form of this condition.

A 2010 article in the journal *Gastroenterology & Hepatology* notes that about 40 percent of people with type 1 diabetes and 30 percent of people with type 2 diabetes may experience some level of delayed gastric emptying.

However, Johns Hopkins states that while impaired vagus nerve function may be part of the cause of gastroparesis in people with diabetes, it's possible diabetes isn't the sole cause. Unfortunately, research hasn't yet determined all of the mechanisms of delayed gastric emptying in people with diabetes, and research remains ongoing.

Having diabetes and gastroparesis presents a challenge, because blood sugar management is such an important part of controlling diabetes. Unfortunately, due to issues associated with delayed stomach emptying, people who have gastroparesis often demonstrate poor blood sugar control. Therefore, it is essential that you follow a diabetic diet that also works for your gastroparesis. Minimizing refined sugars, eating low-carbohydrate meals, and avoiding processed foods can help with blood sugar management. UW Health of the University of Wisconsin recommends carrying "quick-sugar food" to treat low blood sugar so that the food will be absorbed in your mouth rather than your stomach. Work with a registered dietitian or your physician to develop a gastroparesis eating plan that can help you manage your blood sugar. You can also use recipes in this cookbook that have fewer than 10 grams of carbohydrates per serving to help you manage your blood sugar.

The American College of Gastroenterology also recommends:

- Improve glycemic control via diet and medications
- Work with a dietitian
- Eat frequent, small meals low in fiber and fat
- Track your symptoms and foods that may affect blood sugar
- Stick to a daily routine
- Track daily blood glucose levels

If you have diabetes and gastroparesis, it is important for you to monitor your blood glucose consistently in order to ensure you have it under control.

Professionals Who Can Help

Because of the nature of gastroparesis, seeking professional help is essential in managing your condition. You may require a team of health-care providers. Please see the Resources section on page 192 for more information.

PRIMARY CARE PHYSICIAN

Your primary care physician serves as the quarterback for your overall health. He or she paints the big picture of your health, helping you find appropriate specialists and other providers to manage your condition.

INTERNAL MEDICINE SPECIALIST (INTERNIST)

Internists care for the whole patient and may be specialists in different types of internal medicine such as gastroenterology. Seek a board-certified internist through the American Board of Internal Medicine.

GASTROENTEROLOGIST

Gastroenterologists are specialists in diseases of the digestive system. They have specialized training in diseases like gastroparesis, and can provide diagnosis and treatment, as well as suggesting lifestyle modifications to minimize symptoms. Seek a gastroenterologist who is certified in gastroenterology by the American Board of Internal Medicine.

ENDOCRINOLOGIST

If your gastroparesis is related to diabetes or another endocrine condition such as hypothyroidism, working with an endocrinologist is essential. Endocrinologists are doctors specializing in treatment of hormonal imbalances, diseases, and disorders. Look for a certified endocrinologist through the American Board of Internal Medicine.

REGISTERED DIETITIAN

Registered dietitians have specialized knowledge in nutrition and food. They can help you develop an eating plan to manage your dietary needs for any and all conditions you may have. Registered dietitians should have a degree in dietary sciences from an accredited college and receive accreditation via the Accreditation Council for Education in Nutrition and Dietetics of the Academy of Nutrition and Dietetics.

FUNCTIONAL MEDICINE SPECIALIST

Functional medicine specialists integrate holistic practices, seeking the underlying causes of conditions instead of just treating symptoms. Functional medicine specialists may integrate a variety of modalities in treatment that involve body, mind, and spirit. Functional medicine specialists, in conjunction with other health-care providers, may be able to help you develop a lifestyle that minimizes your gastroparesis symptoms.

MENTAL HEALTH-CARE PROFESSIONALS

Chronic, painful illness can lead to a host of emotional and mental changes. You may feel depressed by your diagnosis, you may develop anxiety or phobias surrounding food, or you may just need a sounding board. Finding a licensed mental health-care professional, such as a psychologist, counselor, or life coach, can help you work through any issues associated with your gastroparesis.

ALTERNATIVE CARE PROVIDERS

In conjunction with appropriate medical care, some people also seek care from alternative practitioners to help ease symptoms and anxiety and address nutritional deficiencies or underlying causes of disease. Some alternative practitioners that may be able to help with your gastroparesis include:

- Hypnotists, who can provide hypnosis to help relieve stress and manage symptoms.
- Acupuncturists, who can perform acupuncture that may result in improved symptoms according to the International Foundation for Functional Gastrointestinal Disorders (IFFGD).
- Biofeedback practitioners, who, according to the Mayo Clinic, may help you manage your own symptoms of gastroparesis.

2

EMPOWERED EATING AND HEALTHY LIVING

There's an often-quoted adage: *You are what you eat from your head to your feet.* More and more, science is showing this to be true. The foods you eat and the nutrients you provide to your body play a significant role in your health. For someone with a condition like gastroparesis, this is especially true. What you eat can help you manage the symptoms of your condition.

Alleviating Gastroparesis with Smart Eating

How do you eat smart with gastroparesis? While there are no "right" or "wrong" foods, there are certainly foods that will contribute to symptoms and others that may help you avoid them. Choosing foods that can help you avoid symptoms can go a long way to managing your condition.

During severe symptom flare-ups, stick with a liquid diet. According to Gastroparesis Patient Association for Cures and Treatments, Inc. (G-PACT), when you are experiencing severe nausea and vomiting associated with your gastroparesis, you should consume calorically dense liquids such as broth or bouillon and clear sweetened liquids, such as sports drinks. These will provide your body with energy from calories as well as essential fluids and electrolytes to help you avoid dehydration. Try any of the bone broths listed in Chapter 10 (see page 141), which contain nutrients and electrolytes to provide your body with nutrition while minimizing stomach and intestinal irritation.

As symptoms ease, eat a limited diet of low-residue, liquid, or puréed foods. This includes mild, low-fiber, well-cooked, low-fat foods such as broths with well-cooked vegetables and rice, low-fat/low-fiber crackers, low-fiber cereals, strained fruit juices, and low-fat dairy or nondairy yogurts and milks.

Avoid high-fiber foods. Foods that are very high in fiber may delay stomach emptying, which can contribute to symptoms. Likewise, certain types of fiber may contribute to the formation of bezoars (see "Beware of Bezoars?" on page 28) in certain people. Opt for between 10 and 15 grams of fiber per day (or less, if fiber significantly contributes to your symptoms). The University of Virginia Digestive Health Center recommends avoiding or minimizing consumption of the following high-fiber foods if you have gastroparesis:

- Cruciferous vegetables
- Dried fruits
- High-fiber grains, such as corn, bran, wheat germ, shredded wheat cereal, granola, oats
- Legumes, including peanuts, soy, peas, beans, chickpeas, and lentils
- Nuts and seeds, such as chia, flaxseed, sesame seeds, sunflower seeds, hazelnuts, and cashews
- Popcorn
- Raw and unpeeled fruits
- Raw and unpeeled vegetables

Peel and cook fruits and vegetables. Vegetable and fruit peels contain fiber that is difficult to digest. Peeling them and cooking fruits and vegetables well makes the remaining fiber easier to digest. You may need to experiment to see if even certain recommended cooked fruits and vegetables contribute to your symptoms so you can customize the diet to work best for your condition. It's important to tailor the eating plan to your own symptom triggers, since these can vary greatly from person to person.

Eat small, nutrient-dense meals every few hours. According to a study on the effects of meal volume and published in the *American Journal of Physiology*, eating a large meal significantly delayed gastric emptying. Eating smaller meals may help speed gastric emptying in people with gastroparesis. Make sure that the foods you eat are dense in nutrients to give your body the most vitamins and minerals possible per meal. Likewise, large meal size can contribute to GERD symptoms that sometimes plague people with gastroparesis, according to Health.com. The International Foundation for Functional Gastrointestinal Disorders (IFFGD) recommends eating four to six small meals throughout the day (about half the size of a typical meal) to help manage symptoms.

Eat low-fat foods. Studies, including one published in the *Journal of Clinical Endocrinology and Metabolism*, show that ingestion of fat can slow or delay gastric emptying. Therefore, minimizing fat is an important part of managing the condition. It is important to note, though, that your body needs fat to function, so you shouldn't eliminate it completely. UW Health of the University of Wisconsin recommends eating about 40 grams per day, which breaks down to 5 to 10 grams of fat per meal when eating 4 to 8 meals a day.

Chew foods thoroughly. In order to help foods digest more easily, the IFFGD recommends chewing all food thoroughly before swallowing. The more you chew, the easier it is for your stomach to digest the foods and empty.

Consider FODMAPs. Currently, few studies have been conducted on diets for gastroparesis. Most of the information on the subject comes from anecdotally shared information from patients and clients. According to health coach Stephanie Torres in a blog interview by Kate Scarlata, a registered dietitian and FODMAP and IBS expert, some people with gastroparesis may also benefit from a low-FODMAP diet. This is especially true if you also have IBS (irritable bowel syndrome). If you continue to have symptoms—particularly bloating, gas, and pain—even while following a gastroparesis-friendly diet, eliminating FODMAPs may be helpful.

FODMAP is an acronym for certain types of carbohydrates: fermentable oligo-di-monosaccharides and polyols. There are a number of foods that contain FODMAPs, including:

- Apples
- Artichokes
- Asparagus
- Cashews
- Dairy
- Gluten grains (wheat, barley, and rye)
- Honey
- Onions, garlic, and leeks
- Peaches
- Pears
- Tomatoes
- Watermelon

If you believe FODMAPs may be affecting your symptoms, then look for the recipes in this book with a low-FODMAP label.

Avoid red meat. According to the Cleveland Clinic, people with gastroparesis should avoid red meat or tough cuts of meat, which can be particularly difficult to digest. Instead, choose lean proteins such as fish and white meat poultry. This is especially important if you have GERD, as fatty meats can contribute to GERD symptoms.

Don't drink with meals. The Cleveland Clinic also suggests not drinking liquids for 30 minutes before and after eating, as liquids can dilute digestive juices and delay gastric emptying. When you aren't eating, take small sips of water throughout the day. The Cleveland Clinic also recommends avoiding caffeine, alcohol, and carbonation.

Beware of Bezoars?

One of the risks associated with gastroparesis is the development of bezoars, a tightly packed collection of partially digested and undigested matter that forms in the stomach and can't be emptied. While having gastroparesis certainly increases your chance of bezoar formation, a gastroparesis diagnosis doesn't necessarily mean you'll get one. The University of Virginia notes that bezoar formation is associated with certain foods, including:

Apples

Berries

Brussels sprouts

Celery

Coconuts

Figs

Green beans

Oranges

Persimmons

Potato peels

Pumpkins

Prunes

Raisins

Avoiding these foods can help you avoid formation of bezoars. You can also strain pulp from juices, peel fruits and vegetables, and cook fruits and vegetables extremely well. By taking care with your diet, you will minimize your risks of complicating your gastroparesis with a bezoar.

THE RECIPES IN THIS BOOK

All of the recipes in this book meet the preceding guidelines. They are low in fat with a moderate amount of fiber, and free of indigestible parts that may cause problems. Portion sizes are small in order to facilitate gastric emptying and lower the potential for flare-ups. Many of the recipes also work for people with other conditions (or have tips explaining how to make them work) and may be one or a combination of gluten-free, low-FODMAP, SIBO-friendly, low-sugar, dairy-free, and GERD-friendly. Please see page 51 for an explanation of all of the different recipe labels for special diets.

You may also be able to modify recipes to eliminate the most common food allergens: wheat, dairy, eggs, shellfish, fish, tree nuts, soy, and peanuts. If you have special dietary needs or multiple conditions requiring a unique dietary approach, please seek care from a certified dietitian.

Foods to Enjoy

The foods in this table are excellent in helping you avoid or even alleviate symptoms of gastroparesis. Remember that all foods should be eaten in small portions.

FOOD OR FOOD GROUP	NOTEWORTHY INFORMATION
Almond butter	Limit to 2 tablespoons per day.
Avocado	Use in small amounts because this fruit is fibrous and fatty.
Beverages	These can include water, coconut water, herbal teas, skim milk, and fat-free milk substitutes.
Broths	Make homemade broths from poultry, beef, or fish bones or vegetables.
Dairy (low-fat or nonfat products)	This includes skim milk, low-fat or fat-free plain or Greek yogurt, low-fat cheese, and kefir.
Dairy replacements (low-fat or nonfat)	This includes light coconut milk, rice milk, and almond milk.
Dark, leafy greens	Use small amounts. Remove fibrous parts and cook well. Juice them.
Eggs	Limit use of yolks.
Fish	Remove the skin. If canned, water-packed white-fleshed fish are best.
Fruits	Peel all fruits. Juice fruits, then strain. Cook and strain fruits. Choose soft and low-fiber or watery fruits such as bananas, mango, or melon. Try fruits canned in water (not syrup).
Grains	Choose low-fiber grains such as rice cereal, white bread or low-fiber bread, pasta, and white rice.

▶

Foods to Enjoy continued

FOOD OR FOOD GROUP	NOTEWORTHY INFORMATION
Herbs and spices	Herbs and spices vary depending on tolerance. With FODMAP, GERD, or autoimmune issues, avoid nightshade (chili pepper) spices such as chili powder, paprika, and cayenne. Green herbs, such as oregano, basil, thyme, and chervil all work well. Sea salt has helpful trace minerals. Sweet spices such as cinnamon, nutmeg, allspice, and ginger work well. Try ginger to calm an upset stomach.
Meat and Poultry	Choose very lean ground meats. For poultry, choose skinless white meat, such as chicken or turkey breast. Ground poultry works well.
Mushrooms	Cook well.
Plant protein	Some people are sensitive to soy and vegetable protein, so it's important to test your tolerances to these foods.
Root vegetables	Remove peels and cook well. Purée if desired.
Shellfish and mollusks	This includes shrimp, scallops, clams, mussels, crab, lobster, and crayfish.
Soups	Make low-fat soups with fish or poultry and well-cooked, peeled vegetables, as well as low-fiber grains such as rice or pasta. "Cream" soups are also acceptable when made with skim milk.
Squash	Remove peels, then cook until soft. Use both summer and winter varieties.
Sweeteners	Use natural maple syrup, honey, or stevia.
Tomatoes	Remove skins and juice or cook well. Strain sauces. People with GERD, autoimmune, or FODMAP issues should avoid tomatoes.

Foods to Avoid

While the foods you need to avoid may be highly individual, the following foods may cause problems for many people with gastroparesis.

FOOD OR FOOD GROUP	NOTEWORTHY INFORMATION
Beverages	Coffee if GERD is a problem Caffeinated beverages if GERD is a problem Carbonated beverages if GERD is a problem Alcoholic beverages if GERD is a problem
Coconut	Coconut meat, flaked coconut, and full-fat coconut milk
Cruciferous vegetables	Cauliflower Broccoli Brussels sprouts Cabbage Bok choy
Dairy	High-fat and full-fat dairy, such as cream, ice cream, full-fat milk, sour cream, and full-fat cheese
Dairy substitutes	Soy milk Full-fat coconut milk
Fish	Fish with skin Limit pink or fatty fish
Fruits	Cooked fruits with skins Canned fruits with skins Raw fruits Dried fruits
Garlic	Including garlic powder
Grains	All high-fiber grain products, including corn, bran, shredded wheat cereal, oats, and brown rice
Herbs and spices	Garlic powder Onion powder Pepper Chili pepper spices, such as paprika or cayenne
Legumes and beans	All legumes and beans

▶

Foods to Avoid continued

FOOD OR FOOD GROUP	NOTEWORTHY INFORMATION
Nuts and seeds	All nuts and seeds
Onions	All members of the onion family, including leeks
Peppers	All peppers
Poultry	Eliminate poultry with skin Minimize dark meat poultry
Red meat	All red meats, especially tough cuts.
Root vegetables	Onions Root vegetables with peels Raw root vegetables
Soups	Soups made with heavy cream Soups made with legumes Fatty soups
Tomatoes	Raw tomatoes Tomatoes with skins and seeds
Vegetables	All raw veggies Cooked vegetables with skins or peels

Meeting Your Nutritional Needs

Eating a balanced diet that fulfills all of your body's nutritional needs is challenging when you have gastroparesis. If at all possible, eat small amounts of food more frequently to avoid triggering symptoms that hinder the absorption of the nutrients consumed. Many people with gastroparesis take a few bites of food several times per day.

Nutritionally dense foods are the best way to help your body get the micronutrients (vitamins and minerals), macronutrients (protein, carbohydrates, and fats), and energy (calories) it needs. You need to make sure that the foods you eat count, choosing foods that are higher in calories with plenty of vitamins and minerals. In other words, select whole, healthy, natural foods such as cooked fruits and vegetables, low-fat dairy products, and lean proteins whenever possible.

People with coexisting health conditions, such as diabetes, may have additional issues impeding nutrition. When a person has diabetes, eating the higher-carbohydrate foods that some people with gastroparesis can tolerate, such as juiced fruits, may prove problematic in maintaining blood sugar control. Select lower-carbohydrate foods as well as minimize your intake of sugar, grains, and refined foods.

Consider the following tips for meeting your body's nutritional needs with gastroparesis.

- Minimize processed, empty-calorie foods such as sugary desserts or candy.
- Juice fruits and vegetables to add calories and vitamins without adding fiber, and sip them throughout the day (skip fruit juice if diabetic).
- Make smoothies and shakes from cooked or canned skinless fruits and vegetables, along with liquids such as light coconut milk or juice.
- Add gelatin to increase the protein content of foods.
- Add nonfat milk powder to increase the protein content of foods.
- Fortify soups with vegetable juices or puréed, skinless vegetables.
- Talk to your doctor about supplemental nutrition, through vitamin supplements or a nutritional drink or meal-replacement drink.
- Make peeled root vegetable purées as a side dish and fortify them with nonfat milk powder.
- Choose lower-carbohydrate (less than 10 grams of carbohydrates per serving) options to help control blood sugar.
- Plan meals ahead of time and try to stick to an eating schedule.
- Take gastroparesis-friendly snacks and beverages with you on the go to ensure you get a meal in, even if you're busy.
- Prepare meals ahead of time and freeze them so you have meals ready, even when you're not feeling well.

Voices of Experience

Stephanie Hyatt, a 27-year-old who's had gastroparesis for most of her life, has some words of wisdom for people who are newly diagnosed with gastroparesis:

Gastroparesis is quite the roller coaster. You will learn and accept your new "normal," and it won't be normal compared to people who are healthy. You can't compare your life to others. Everyone has difficulties in life. . . . At times you will feel sad and discouraged, and that's OK to feel that way. It's better expressing and accepting those emotions rather than dismissing and holding them in. If you need to cry for a few hours, do it! Just don't sit and wallow in your misery, because ultimately that will exacerbate the physical symptoms.

You are a lot stronger than you think you are!

To read more from Stephanie, check out her Q&A on page 175 in Appendix B: Stories from the Front Line.

- Sip on nourishing homemade broths throughout the day to provide nutrients and calories.
- Rely heavily on soups and stews that contain plenty of cooked vegetables and lean sources of animal protein for a full, nutritious meal.
- Add a few tablespoons of almond butter to a smoothie to increase protein and calories.

When You're Afraid to Eat

Nearly everyone with gastrointestinal disorders understands the fear that sometimes accompanies even the thought of eating. I get it. When I was living with undiagnosed celiac disease and my symptoms were rampant, I didn't know exactly what foods were causing my symptoms, but I certainly understood that it was eating that triggered them. Some days, the thought of taking a bite of food may feel almost more than you can handle.

Many people with gastroparesis experience a fear of eating, never knowing when doing so is going to trigger an outbreak of symptoms. While this fear is understandable, it is very important for your own good health that you try to eat. Below are some tips for overcoming the fear.

Learn your triggers. Maintain a food/symptoms diary and track what you eat and any symptoms the foods cause. Knowing your triggers can empower you to make choices that will be less likely to cause you to experience symptoms.

Visualize. Before you sit down to eat, if you are feeling fearful, sit quietly and close your eyes. Breathe deeply and visualize yourself eating the food and feeling well afterward.

Admit your fear to yourself or someone else. Admitting that you feel afraid can be the first step in overcoming it. Talk through your fear with another person, or journal about your fear. Create ways to overcome your objections.

Keep a record of the times you eat and don't have symptoms. Refer to this information whenever you start to feel afraid of eating; that way, you can remind yourself that you've eaten successfully many times without triggering symptoms.

Trust yourself. Make a promise to yourself that you will provide only nourishing foods in amounts that don't elicit symptoms—and stick to that commitment in order to build trust in yourself.

Consider talk therapy. Talk with your health-care provider if you have a severe eating phobia. He or she may refer you to someone to help you deal with the anxiety associated with eating.

3

THE GASTROPARESIS MEAL PLAN

Food plays an important role in everyone's health, and the way you eat on a day-to-day and meal-to-meal basis can have a significant impact on how you feel. This is particularly true for people suffering from gastroparesis, as certain ways of eating do appear to impact symptoms. The meal plan in this chapter is designed to help minimize your symptoms, empowering you to live a more balanced and less stressful life. It does so by teaching you to eat in a way that works best for *your* digestive system, thus reducing your dependence on drugs or medical treatments.

Making the Gastroparesis Meal Plan Work for You

Everybody is unique, so it's important that you learn your own triggers and "safe" foods. If you have difficulty with any of the foods in the meal plan, make substitutions that work for you.

This meal plan lays out a simple, two-week plan. Each day contains five small meals, including breakfast, morning snack, lunch, mid-afternoon snack, and dinner, which you can break down further into six or more smaller meals if needed. The plan minimizes preparation time by using leftovers as much as possible for lunches throughout the week. All of the recipes contain affordable, easy-to-find ingredients, are simple to prepare, and require minimal special equipment.

Space meals every two to three hours, and follow the small portion sizes recommended in order to avoid symptom flares while maximizing nutrition and stabilizing blood sugar. It's important that you discuss this meal plan with your doctor or dietitian.

To save time in meal preparation during busy weekdays, consider the following tips:

- Whenever possible, prepare meals and snacks ahead of time.
- Make big batches of food, soups, and stocks on the weekends or in the evening and freeze or refrigerate them for use throughout the week.
- Invest in a slow cooker ($30 to $100). Slow cookers are a great for cooking foods with little intervention. You can get a dish started in the morning and have a hot meal at dinnertime, and often with very little preparation.
- Invest in small, single-serving containers that are freezer- and microwave-safe. Additionally, use resealable plastic bags to apportion individual servings so you can take meals and snacks on the go.
- Pre-cook commonly used ingredients, such as white rice, and freeze them in one-cup servings in resealable plastic bags.

A Typical Day on the Plan

Eating every few hours can seem fairly labor intensive, particularly when you have to prepare foods from scratch. Here's a typical schedule that you may want to adopt or adapt to support your own eating needs.

6 a.m.	Wake up, shower, get ready for the day
7 to 7:45 a.m.	Prepare and eat breakfast
10:30 a.m.	Eat a morning snack
12:30 p.m.	Eat lunch
3:30 p.m.	Eat an afternoon snack
5:30 to 6:45 p.m.	Prepare and eat dinner
7:30 p.m.	Prepare any meals or snacks for the next day

Kitchen Equipment and Pantry List

A well-prepared kitchen provides enough equipment and pantry staples to allow you to make these simple meals.

ESSENTIAL EQUIPMENT

To make the recipes in this book, you'll need the following essential equipment.

Blender

A blender is essential for making smoothies and purées. Many people feel like they need a very powerful blender, like a Vitamix, which is expensive. While a Vitamix blender is great, a much less expensive blender, such as a Ninja, can work well. You can even use an immersion blender (stick blender) or a food processor.

Colanders/Sieves

A medium or large fine-mesh sieve and a colander with larger holes will help you strain juices and other foods.

Dutch Oven or Stockpot

A large pot is ideal for making soups and stews. Choose one that is sturdy and can go from the stovetop to the oven.

Pots

Ideally, you will need pots in small, medium, and large sizes. Make sure the pots all have lids that fit tightly.

Sauté Pans

You will benefit from having a few different sauté pans. At least one should be a large (10- to 12-inch) nonstick sauté pan, and another should be ovenproof (no plastic handles!).

Slow Cooker

A slow cooker is an essential piece of kitchen equipment, especially if you plan to make lots of broths, soups, and stews. Choose one with a crock that you can take out of its housing and wash or store in the refrigerator.

Vegetable Peeler

Since you need to peel all fruits and vegetables before using them, a vegetable peeler is one of the most essential pieces of equipment in your kitchen.

Miscellaneous

You'll also need a lot of miscellaneous equipment that you may already have in your kitchen, such as cutting boards, measuring cups and spoons, wooden spoons, rubber spatulas, and mixing bowls.

PANTRY STAPLES

A well-stocked pantry can help you be more successful on your gastroparesis meal plan. Having the right ingredients on hand allows you to make meals quickly and easily. Items to keep in your pantry include:

Canned/Packaged Goods

100 percent fruit juice
Canned clams
Canned cooked vegetables
Canned peeled fruits in juice (not syrup)
Dried mushrooms
Herbal teas
Light coconut milk
Low-fat almond milk
Low-fat broths
Low-fat rice milk
Tomato juice
Unsweetened applesauce
Water-packed tuna

Condiments

Apple cider vinegar
Balsamic vinegar
Dijon mustard
Fat-free mayonnaise
Red wine vinegar

Dairy

Nonfat milk
Plain nonfat yogurt or Greek yogurt
Unsalted butter

Dry Goods

Almond meal (for almond milk)
Arrowroot powder
Bread/breadcrumbs
Cream of Wheat (farina)
Gelatin powder
Nonfat milk powder
Pasta or gluten-free pasta
Quinoa
Sweet rice flour
White or gluten-free flour
White rice

Dried Herbs and Spices

Alcohol-free vanilla extract
Allspice
Cinnamon
Cloves
Coriander
Cumin
Dried chervil
Dried marjoram
Dried oregano
Dried tarragon
Dried thyme
Ground ginger
Nutmeg
Salt

Frozen Foods

Boneless skinless chicken breasts
Boneless skinless turkey breasts
Bones (beef, poultry, or fish for making stock)
Fish fillets
Fruits
Nonfat ice cream
Shellfish
Vegetables

Oils

Coconut oil
Extra-virgin olive oil

Snack Foods

Baby foods
Low-fat, low-fiber crackers
Saltines

Sweeteners

Honey
Liquid stevia
Pure maple syrup

Other Staples

Baby spinach
Berries
Carrots
Eggs
Fresh ginger
Lemons
Limes
Oranges
Potatoes
Scallions
Silken tofu
Sweet potatoes
Zucchini

Setting Yourself Up for Success

It's not always easy to make huge dietary changes, even when you understand there will be long-term benefits that affect how you feel. I understand this perfectly. Even though I knew gluten made me very ill, it took me months to actually get serious about getting it out of my diet. The thought of all that change can feel daunting and difficult. After a while, however, shopping and cooking to support your health will become second nature.

It's natural to feel some apprehension about having to make such a major dietary overhaul. However, with persistence and some strategies for success, it will soon feel like second nature to you as well.

COOK AHEAD

Whenever possible, cook ahead of time and freeze foods. That way, you'll always have the foods you need when you need them. Make a big pot of broth one or two times per week, and freeze it in one-cup containers, labeled with the type of broth and the date you made it. Do this with other recipe ingredients and meals that you might need during particularly busy weeks, as well.

USE A SLOW COOKER

My slow cooker is in almost continual operation during the week. When I'm not making stock, I make simple things like applesauce, spaghetti squash, soups, and stews in my slow cooker, tossing ingredients in first thing in the morning and arriving home to a warm meal that night. Be sure to freeze leftovers or use them for lunches.

Gastroparesis-Friendly Pantry Substitutions

REMOVE	REPLACE WITH
Heavy cream, whole milk	Nonfat milk, nonfat milk powder, almond milk, light coconut milk
Sour cream	Nonfat plain Greek yogurt
Full-fat coconut milk	Light coconut milk
Fruit on the bottom yogurt	Nonfat plain Greek yogurt, nonfat plain yogurt, nondairy low-fat plain yogurt (such as coconut yogurt or almond yogurt)
Orange juice with pulp	Strained orange juice
Tomato sauce	Strained tomato sauce, strained tomato juice
Canned tomatoes	Strained tomato sauce, tomato juice
Fruits in syrup	Peeled fruits in 100 percent juice
White sugar	Liquid stevia, honey, pure maple syrup
Brown rice	White rice
Oatmeal	Cream of Wheat (farina), white rice
Ground beef	Ground turkey breast, ground chicken breast
Red meat	Fish, white meat skinless poultry, shellfish
Canned broth	Homemade stocks (see page 147)
Full-fat mayonnaise	Avocado, Dijon mustard, nonfat plain yogurt
Canned legumes	Fresh vegetables
High-fiber cereals	Low-fiber, low-sugar cereals such as crisped rice or Cream of Wheat (farina)
Cornstarch	Arrowroot powder
White flour (if gluten-sensitive)	Gluten-free flour, sweet rice flour, potato starch flour
Corn syrup	Honey, liquid stevia, pure maple syrup
Sweetened applesauce	Unsweetened strained applesauce, or homemade applesauce
Chili powder	Cumin, coriander
Pasta (if gluten-sensitive)	Gluten-free pasta, homemade zucchini noodles
Raw fruits	Peeled and cooked strained fruits
Raw vegetables	Peeled and cooked vegetables

REMOVE TEMPTATIONS FROM THE HOUSE (OR SEGREGATE THEM)

Get rid of foods in the house that aren't going to benefit your meal plan. For example, I discovered how much easier it was to go gluten-free and dairy-free when my son left for college. With all of his gluten and dairy foods around the house, I was constantly tempted and occasionally caved. With him out of the house, suddenly gluten-free was much easier—because there was nothing there to tempt me.

If you share your home with other people who don't share your dietary restrictions, then I suggest segregating your foods from theirs. If possible, put their foods in a separate cupboard or freezer that you don't use. That way, they won't constantly be in your line of sight, inviting you to partake.

PLAN YOUR MEALS

Use the meal plans here or make up your own. Stick with the meals and snacks you have planned that week, and follow your plan exactly.

SHOP WITH A LIST

Avoid temptations at the grocery store by shopping from a list. List only the items you need for meals or snacks that week.

COOK ONCE, EAT TWICE (OR MORE)

Because I make everything from scratch in my house, I've discovered that I like to make big batches of food and freeze leftovers or eat them for lunches (or even breakfasts) in the days that follow. Cooking dinner with the intention of having it carry over to one or two meals in the following days means you will be cooking only about every other day. This saves tons of time in the kitchen.

TRACK YOUR SYMPTOMS

Keep a journal of the foods you eat and any symptoms you experience. Once you start feeling better, it's pretty easy to forget how lousy you used to feel, which makes slipping up easier. Your food and symptom journal can remind you how much better you feel. In other words, keeping a journal can keep you on track.

Voices of Experience

Nikki Weber, a young professional who was diagnosed with gastroparesis five years ago, shares her tips for living a "normal" life with gastroparesis:

I have learned that it's best if I suggest places for my friends and me, since I can pick places that fit my needs, too. For example, rather than go to a restaurant and watch my friends eat, I will suggest a self-serve frozen yogurt place that has sorbet options, or a Starbucks where I can sip on a drink and easily take the rest of it to go. I have also worked to make my apartment the "hang out" spot with my friends. This works great on days when I am exhausted because I can invite people over for a movie, but still stay in my pajamas and have all my comforts of home (like my medicine and heating pad!).

To read more from Nikki, check out her Q&A on page 181 in Appendix B: Stories from the Front Line. You can find also find her recipe for vegan smoothies on page 64.

YOUR TWO-WEEK MEAL PLAN

WEEK ONE	BREAKFAST	MORNING SNACK	LUNCH	AFTERNOON SNACK	DINNER
Monday	Yogurt with Blueberry Sauce	Almond Joy Smoothie	Turkey-Ginger Soup	Winter Squash–Ginger Spread Saltines	Orange-Tarragon Scallops Creamed Spinach
Tuesday	Leftover Almond Joy Smoothie	Cream Cheese and Herb Spread Saltines	Leftover Turkey-Ginger Soup	Leftover Winter Squash–Ginger Spread Saltines	Chicken-Lime Stew
Wednesday	Apple-Almond Cream of Rice Cereal	Summer Squash and Lemon Dip or Spread Saltines	Leftover Chicken-Lime Stew	Leftover Cream Cheese and Herb Spread Crackers	Spinach Quiche
Thursday	Mellow Green Smoothie	¼ cup plain yogurt with 1 tablespoon honey and ¼ sliced banana	Leftover Spinach Quiche	Leftover Summer Squash and Lemon Dip or Spread Saltines	Coconut Shrimp Chowder
Friday	Leftover Spinach Quiche	Leftover Mellow Green Smoothie	Baked Fish Sticks Applesauce	Leftover Coconut Shrimp Chowder	Spaghetti Squash with Turkey-Tomato Sauce
Saturday	Poached Eggs over Sweet Potato Hash	Tropical Smoothie	Leftover Spaghetti Squash	Leftover Baked Fish Sticks	Shrimp and "Grits" Maple–Butternut Squash Purée
Sunday	Leftover Tropical Smoothie	Toast, with 1 tablespoon almond butter	Leftover Shrimp and "Grits"	Orange-Cranberry Gelatin	Cod Poached in Tomato Sauce Leftover Maple–Butternut Squash Purée

YOUR TWO-WEEK MEAL PLAN

WEEK TWO	BREAKFAST	MORNING SNACK	LUNCH	AFTERNOON SNACK	DINNER
Monday	Mushroom and Thyme Scrambled Eggs	Leftover Orange-Cranberry Gelatin	Leftover Cod Poached in Tomato Sauce	Creamy Apple-Ginger Smoothie	Cream of Mushroom Soup
Tuesday	Shrimp and Spinach Frittata	Leftover Creamy Apple-Ginger Smoothie	Leftover Cream of Mushroom Soup	Creamy Hot Chai Drink	Fish Stew
Wednesday	Yogurt with Blueberry Sauce	Leftover Shrimp and Spinach Frittata	Leftover Fish Stew	Sweet Potato Fries	Baked Mushroom Risotto
Thursday	Vanilla-Orange French Toast	Mellow Green Smoothie	Leftover Baked Mushroom Risotto	Cheesy Mashed Potatoes	Halibut with Lemon and Dill Root Vegetable Purée
Friday	Avocado and Herb Omelet	Leftover Mellow Green Smoothie	Leftover Halibut with Lemon and Dill Leftover Root Vegetable Purée	Plain nonfat yogurt Canned peaches	Butternut Squash Soup
Saturday	Acorn Squash and Egg Bake	Leftover Butternut Squash Soup	Tomato and Vegetable Soup	Cream Cheese and Herb Spread	Steamer Clams with Rice Creamed Spinach
Sunday	Apple-Almond Cream of Rice Cereal	Almond Joy Smoothie	Carrot-Ginger Soup	Leftover Tomato and Vegetable Soup	Asparagus Quiche

ENLIST THE HELP OF FRIENDS AND FAMILY

Explaining your condition to the people you'll be sharing meals with is important, as is discussing how food impacts how you feel. When your family and friends understand what you need, it will be easier to negotiate mealtimes, and they can encourage you to stay on track. Sharing pertinent information will also make social occasions, where food may be an issue, easier to manage. If a friend does invite you to a meal or gathering, offer to make something to bring to share so you'll know you have something you can eat.

Lifelong Advice for Gastroparesis Sufferers

While dietary modifications are important to manage your gastroparesis, you may also need to make some lifestyle modifications to live your best life.

MANAGE STRESS

Life can be stressful, even when you don't have a chronic condition. However, when you do have a condition such as gastroparesis, managing stress is even more essential, because it helps keep your body's hormonal levels normal and allows your body adequate resources to support optimal health. To better manage stress:

- Engage in regular moderate exercise, such as walking, swimming, or yoga.

- Practice stress-release techniques, such as meditation or yoga.

- Get plenty of sleep.

- Go someplace quiet for a moment when you do feel stressed. Close your eyes, and breathe deeply.

- Eliminate unnecessary stressors from your life.

EXERCISE REGULARLY

Exercise lowers stress, anxiety, and depression levels. When you exercise, neurohormones are produced, which are associated with improving not only your mood but also learning. An added benefit is that moderate exercise can help increase how quickly your stomach empties. Consider mild exercise, such as regular daily walks or other low-impact activity.

QUIT SMOKING

Smoking can alter how your stomach empties, so it is important that you quit smoking or using tobacco products. If you need help, talk to your doctor about strategies for quitting.

MAINTAIN REGULAR SLEEP PATTERNS

Whenever you deal with chronic illness, sleep is essential in maintaining energy levels and controlling both pain and stress. Sleeping consistent hours (at the same time) every night can help normalize sleep patterns, allowing you to sleep better. Other tips for better sleep:

- Control the climate in your room so you're not too hot or cold.

- Go to bed at the same time every night and rise at the same time every morning.

- If you need it, take a 20- to 30-minute nap during the day.
- Avoid screens (smartphones, computers, etc.) about an hour before bedtime.
- Engage in a bedtime ritual, such as bathing and reading right before bed. A bedtime ritual can help your body know it's time to sleep.
- Keep your room as dark as possible.

WATCH YOUR POSTURE

Your posture can affect the speed of gastric emptying. Avoid lying or slouching for at least an hour after eating. Instead, sit upright, stand, or walk.

PRACTICE SELF-CARE

Chronic illness can be stressful and painful, so it's important that you care for yourself as much as possible. Treat yourself to a massage from time to time, or spend time engaging in activities that make you feel good or bring you pleasure.

SEEK SUPPORT

Ask your friends and family for support. Likewise, it may be helpful to seek the support of others who truly understand what you are going through. There are a number of gastroparesis advocacy organizations and groups, such as G-PACT and the Digestive Health Alliance (DHA), which can allow you to connect with others who truly understand your condition and its challenges. You'll find information on where to find these and other support groups for gastroparesis in the Resource section of this book on page 192.

Voices of Experience

Ashley Jenkins, a college student who was diagnosed with gastroparesis in 2011, shares her tips for living well with gastroparesis:

One self-care tip is to get enough sleep. I know it's hard sometimes, but exhaustion just makes gastroparesis worse. . . . Another self-care tip is to join support groups. Facebook has a ton of groups. I even created a group to share GP-friendly recipes. These groups not only build friendships; they can teach you a lot and help you brainstorm more ways to help yourself. Finally, as annoying as it can be, when you first discover you have gastroparesis it is really helpful to keep a food journal and figure out which foods work well and which don't. . . . our bodies react differently so you have to experiment. . . .

To read more from Ashley, check out her Q&A on page 184 in Appendix B: Stories from the Front Line. To check out Ashley's Facebook group, see Resources, page 193.

EAT THE HIGHEST QUALITY FOOD YOU CAN AFFORD

Try to seek high-quality sources of food, such as local organic farmers and ranchers. Consider visiting local farmer's markets or farm stands, and find sellers who offer eggs from organic, cage-free chickens. To find local farmers, visit EatWild.com, and see Appendix D: The Dirty Dozen and the Clean Fifteen (page 187) for a list of the foods that contain the highest levels of pesticide residue.

REMEMBER THAT YOU'RE A PERSON, NOT A DIAGNOSIS

People with chronic illness can sometimes fall into the trap of thinking of themselves as primarily a diagnosis. While your diagnosis is necessary for seeking appropriate treatment, remember that you are so much more than your gastroparesis, and seek to live the fullest, most balanced life possible.

Defensive Dining: Eating Out with Gastroparesis

When you're on a very restricted diet, dining out can be fraught with peril. I discovered early in my celiac diagnosis that I often grew ill after eating in restaurants, even when I carefully outlined exactly what I couldn't eat (gluten or dairy). Here are some tips for managing dining-out situations.

Ask lots of questions. Developing a rapport with your server is essential to avoiding foods you can't eat. I always explain to my server that I have food allergies (using the word *allergies* is very important, because restaurants want to avoid liability and tend to be very careful about food allergies) and then ask questions about specific menu items.

Go Off-Menu. If you're not satisfied that the menu items will meet your specific dietary needs, ask about ordering off the menu, such as a piece of fish or poultry and some steamed vegetables without oil or seasonings.

LEARN AS MUCH AS YOU CAN

It is important that you learn as much as you can about your condition so you can advocate for yourself. Seek information from reliable organizations (see Resources on page 192). Find physicians who are knowledgeable and known for treating gastroparesis and work closely with them to obtain the best possible care. Stay informed and up-to-date on the latest research about gastroparesis and developments in care and treatment so that you can get the best care available.

Enlist the aid of your server. Always be very polite to your server and offer thanks (and a good tip) after he or she helped meet your dietary needs. G-PACT offers Restaurant Cards (www.g-pact.org/patient-resources) to share with your server requesting special food items, so it may be a good idea to carry a card with you.

Go to restaurants during off-peak hours. Both your server and the chef are much more likely to have the time and ability to accommodate you when they aren't super busy.

Skip the sauce. Sauces are often a source of hidden fats and spices. Ask for plain fish or steamed vegetables without seasonings.

Order clear soups or broths. Avoid cream soups or chowders, which tend to be high in fat.

Ask if you can order off the children's or senior's menus. These menus feature much smaller portion sizes. Alternatively, ask for a to-go box right away and put most of the food away for later.

Take your own food. When invited to parties or dinner gatherings, explain to the host your dietary restrictions and ask if you can bring a dish to share. Then, bring something that you can eat and stick with that.

PART TWO

The
Recipes

The recipes in the following chapters are labeled to help you determine which are appropriate for your specific dietary needs. Recipe labels include the following:

GLUTEN-FREE — These recipes have no gluten-containing ingredients, so they work well for people who don't eat gluten or have celiac disease.

DAIRY-FREE — These recipes contain no dairy products of any kind, nor do they contain either of the major components of dairy products, casein and lactose.

LOW-FODMAP — These recipes are good for people who suffer irritable bowel syndrome (IBS) or small intestine bacterial overgrowth (SIBO). Minimizing FODMAPs may help control bloating, gas, and other intestinal symptoms.

LOW-CARB — These recipes contain fewer than 10 grams of carbohydrates per serving. They also have no processed grains or any type of added sugar in the recipe.

LOW-SUGAR — These recipes contain fewer than 5 grams of sugar per serving.

SIBO-FRIENDLY — These recipes are those that can help you control bacterial overgrowth after treatment for SIBO. They are low in fructose and another type of carbohydrate called fructans.

GERD-FRIENDLY — These recipes are low in acid, fat, and spices that may trigger outbreaks of gastroesophageal reflux disease or heartburn.

4

DRINKS & SMOOTHIES

Ginger Fizz

GLUTEN-FREE | DAIRY-FREE | LOW-FODMAP | LOW-CARB
LOW-SUGAR | SIBO-FRIENDLY | GERD-FRIENDLY

This is a great alternative to commercially prepared ginger ale, which many people find settles their stomach. Make a glass and sip this beverage throughout the day to combat nausea. The recipe uses all-natural ingredients and has 0 grams of sugar, making it friendly for people with diabetes.

SERVES 1
Serving size: 8 ounces
Prep time: 5 minutes
Cook time: None

———————

1-inch piece peeled fresh ginger
1 cup cold sparkling mineral water
2 to 3 drops liquid stevia

Substitution Tip: Feel free to add more or less ginger, or make the fizz sweeter or less sweet by varying how many drops of stevia you add. If you tolerate lemon well, squeeze the juice of half a lemon or orange through a mesh sieve into the beverage to add some vitamin C. If you have GERD, do not add the lemon or orange juice.

1. Using a rasp-style grater, grate the peeled ginger and put it in a piece of cheesecloth.

2. Wrap the cheesecloth around the ginger and hold it above a drinking glass.

3. Squeeze the cheesecloth so that the juice from the ginger drips into the glass.

4. Add the mineral water and stevia, and stir together.

 PER SERVING CALORIES: 1; PROTEIN: 0G; TOTAL FAT: 0G; SATURATED FAT: 0G; CARBOHYDRATES: 0G; SUGAR: 0G; FIBER: 0G; SODIUM: 0MG

Ginger Nausea Tea

GLUTEN-FREE | DAIRY-FREE | LOW-FODMAP | LOW-CARB
LOW-SUGAR | SIBO-FRIENDLY | GERD-FRIENDLY

Hot ginger tea is another nausea fighter. This version is very simple to make, and you can adjust the sweetness or add other flavors as needed. If a hot beverage is more soothing to your stomach than a cool one, then sip on a cup of this tea to calm your nausea.

SERVES 1
Serving size: 8 ounces
Prep time: 5 minutes
Cook time: 5 minutes

———

1-inch piece grated peeled fresh ginger
1 cup hot water
1 to 2 drops liquid stevia (optional)

Cooking Tip: Ginger is pulpy, so it can be difficult to grate. If you have a food processor, you can first cut the peeled ginger root into smaller chunks and then pulse them in the food processor for 5 to 10 one-second pulses instead of grating it.

1. Place the grated ginger in a glass measuring cup.

2. Add the hot water and allow the ginger to steep for at least 5 minutes.

3. Add the stevia (if using) to sweeten.

4. Strain the liquid through a fine-mesh sieve into a mug.

 PER SERVING CALORIES: 1; PROTEIN: 0G; TOTAL FAT: 0G; SATURATED FAT: 0G; CARBOHYDRATES: 0G; SUGAR: 0G; FIBER: 0G; SODIUM: 0MG

Rice Milk

GLUTEN-FREE | DAIRY-FREE | LOW-FODMAP | SIBO-FRIENDLY | GERD-FRIENDLY

If you're allergic to cow's milk, homemade rice milk makes an easy and flavorful substitute. It is soothing to the stomach, low in FODMAPs, and makes an excellent milk replacement for smoothies. Rice is relatively high in carbohydrates, so if you're diabetic this beverage may not be the best dairy alternative. See the recipe for Almond Milk that follows for a diabetic-friendly, nondairy milk. This rice milk will keep in the refrigerator for up to a week.

SERVES 5

Serving size: ½ cup

Prep time: 5 minutes

Cook time: None

———————

1 cup cooked white rice

4 cups cold water

Pinch sea salt

1 to 2 drops stevia (optional)

Substitution Tip: If you find the taste of stevia unpleasant, you can omit it altogether or replace it with 1 to 2 teaspoons of honey. Honey isn't FODMAP-friendly, however; so if you are avoiding FODMAPs, then stick with the stevia.

Put all of the ingredients, including the stevia (if using), in a blender. Process on high for 4 minutes.

 PER SERVING CALORIES: 68; PROTEIN: 1G; TOTAL FAT: 0G; SATURATED FAT: 0G; CARBOHYDRATES: 15G; SUGAR: 0G; FIBER: 0G; SODIUM: 48MG

Almond Milk

GLUTEN-FREE | DAIRY-FREE | LOW-FODMAP | LOW-CARB
LOW-SUGAR | SIBO-FRIENDLY | GERD-FRIENDLY

This nondairy milk alternative is very low in carbohydrates, making it a good choice for people with diabetes. Because the almonds and fiber are filtered out, the resulting milk is not likely to irritate your gastroparesis symptoms. Almond milk makes a great base for vegan smoothies and will keep in the refrigerator for up to four days.

SERVES 6
Serving size: 4 ounces
Prep time: 10 minutes
Cook time: None

———

1 cup raw almonds
3 cups water, plus more for soaking
Pinch sea salt (optional)
1 to 2 drops liquid stevia (optional)

Cooking Tip: A nut milk bag can also be used to strain the almond milk. They can be found online and in many specialty cooking stores. Pour the unfiltered almond milk through the bag and squeeze it, moving from the top to the bottom of the bag (almost like milking a cow) to obtain the milk.

1. Put the almonds in a medium bowl and cover them with cold water. Let the almonds soak for 12 hours.

2. Drain the almonds, discarding the water used for soaking, and put the nuts in a blender.

3. Add the 3 cups of water to the blender, and then add the stevia and salt (if using).

4. Blend on high for 4 minutes.

5. Place a large fine-mesh sieve lined with cheesecloth over a large glass measuring cup. Carefully strain the almond milk through the sieve.

6. Wrap the cheesecloth around the remaining almond meal and gently squeeze it to extract the rest of the liquid.

 PER SERVING CALORIES: 38; PROTEIN: 1G; TOTAL FAT: 3G; SATURATED FAT: 0G; CARBOHYDRATES: 1G; SUGAR: 1G; FIBER: 0G; SODIUM: 0MG

Creamy Hot Chai Drink

GLUTEN-FREE | DAIRY-FREE | LOW-FODMAP | LOW-CARB
LOW-SUGAR | SIBO-FRIENDLY | GERD-FRIENDLY

This creamy chai drink is deliciously aromatic. While this version is dairy-free, if you can tolerate dairy it can also be made with regular milk, and add a few tablespoons of dry milk powder to increase protein intake if you wish. This is the perfect beverage to sip when you're craving something sweet and soothing.

SERVES 2

Serving size: 4 ounces
Prep time: 5 minutes
Cook time: 5 minutes

---

1 cup almond milk (page 57)
1 cinnamon stick
½-inch piece peeled fresh ginger, cut into pieces
2 whole cloves
1 cardamom pod (optional)
2 pieces whole allspice
Dash ground nutmeg
1 to 2 drops liquid stevia

Substitution Tip: If you don't enjoy the taste of stevia, consider adding 1 or 2 teaspoons of pure maple syrup to the tea instead. Be sure to use pure maple syrup and not pancake syrup. If you are on a low-carbohydrate diet, it is important to take the additional carbohydrates from the maple syrup (about 3 grams per teaspoon) into account.

1. In a small saucepan, heat the milk, cinnamon, ginger, cloves, cardamom (if using), allspice, and nutmeg over medium-high heat until the milk simmers. Stir frequently.

2. Remove the mixture from the heat and allow it to steep for 5 minutes.

3. Stir in the stevia.

4. Strain the hot chai drink through a small fine-mesh sieve into mugs.

PER SERVING CALORIES: 21; PROTEIN: 1G; TOTAL FAT: 2G; SATURATED FAT: OG; CARBOHYDRATES: 1G; SUGAR: OG; FIBER: 1G; SODIUM: OMG

Orange-Vanilla Smoothie

This blended orange smoothie is high in vitamin C, calcium, and flavor. It tastes like an Orange Julius and makes a delicious morning meal. The fat-free milk powder adds protein, making the smoothie satisfying. Be certain to use 100 percent real juice and not an orange-flavored beverage, which likely contains added sugar.

SERVES 4

Serving size: 4 ounces
Prep time: 5 minutes
Cook time: None

———

½ cup orange juice

½ cup nonfat milk

1 cup crushed ice

2 tablespoons nonfat dry milk powder

½ teaspoon alcohol-free vanilla extract

Ingredient Tip: The most flavorful orange juice is freshly squeezed. If you have any kind of a citrus juicer or any other type of a juicer, then squeeze your own orange juice whenever you can.

1. Strain the juice through a fine-mesh sieve to remove any pulp.

2. Combine all ingredients in a blender.

3. Blend on high for 1 to 2 minutes, until smooth.

PER SERVING CALORIES: 29; PROTEIN: 1G; TOTAL FAT: 0G; SATURATED FAT: 0G; CARBOHYDRATES: 5G; SUGAR: 5G; FIBER: 0G; SODIUM: 20MG

Creamy Apple-Ginger Smoothie

GLUTEN-FREE

Ginger and apples are a delicious and classic flavor combination. This simple smoothie incorporates low-fat yogurt, which adds protein and calcium and gives the smoothie a creamy texture. Cinnamon and nutmeg add sweetness to this tasty beverage. The smoothie will keep for up to three days in the refrigerator.

SERVES 4

Serving size: 4 ounces

Prep time: 5 minutes

Cook time: None

―――――――

½ cup cold apple juice

½ cup nonfat milk

1 cup nonfat plain yogurt

¼ teaspoon ground ginger

¼ teaspoon ground cinnamon

Pinch ground nutmeg

Ingredient Tip: To make this smoothie dairy-free, replace the nonfat milk with the Almond Milk on page 57 and use a nondairy cultured yogurt (such as almond or coconut yogurt) in place of the yogurt.

Combine all of the ingredients in a blender. Blend on high for 1 or 2 minutes, until smooth.

 PER SERVING CALORIES: 64; PROTEIN: 4G; TOTAL FAT: 0G; SATURATED FAT: 0G; CARBOHYDRATES: 12G; SUGAR: 9G; FIBER: 0G; SODIUM: 65MG

Mellow Green Smoothie

GLUTEN-FREE | DAIRY-FREE | LOW-FODMAP | LOW-CARB | LOW-SUGAR

This recipe calls for frozen, cooked spinach, although you can also use fresh, raw spinach if you tolerate raw greens well. The almond butter adds protein along with the almond milk. Cinnamon, melon, and liquid stevia add a touch of sweetness to counteract any bitterness of the spinach. This beverage will keep in the refrigerator for up to three days.

SERVES 4

Serving size: 4 ounces

Prep time: 5 minutes

Cook time: None

———

¼ cup chopped honeydew melon

¼ cup chopped frozen spinach

1 tablespoon almond butter

½ cup Almond Milk (page 57)

2 to 3 drops liquid stevia

¼ teaspoon ground cinnamon

Ingredient Tip: You can make and freeze your own frozen spinach. Bring a large pot of water to a boil. Add about 4 ounces chopped spinach and cook for 1 minute. Drain and allow the spinach to cool before freezing. Make a large batch and put ¼ cup of the cooked spinach in individual ziplock bags to freeze and use another day.

Combine all of the ingredients in a blender and blend on high for 2 to 3 minutes, until smooth.

PER SERVING CALORIES: 33; PROTEIN: 1G; TOTAL FAT: 3G; SATURATED FAT: 0G; CARBOHYDRATES: 2G; SUGAR: 1G; FIBER: 0G; SODIUM: 3MG

Almond Joy Smoothie

GLUTEN-FREE | DAIRY-FREE | LOW-FODMAP | LOW-CARB
LOW-SUGAR | SIBO-FRIENDLY | GERD-FRIENDLY

The light coconut milk and coconut yogurt in this smoothie are a mild flavor, while the almond butter hints at the taste of a candy bar and adds protein. Be sure to use canned light coconut milk—the full-fat variety has too much fat and could delay gastric emptying.

SERVES 4

Serving size: 4 ounces
Prep time: 5 minutes
Cook time: None

½ cup light coconut milk
½ cup nonfat, plain cultured
    coconut yogurt
2 tablespoons almond butter
1 to 2 drops liquid stevia

Substitution Tip: If you're not a fan of coconut milk or don't tolerate it well, then replace it with the Almond Milk (page 57) and replace the coconut yogurt with almond yogurt. If you tolerate dairy well, you can also substitute traditional dairy products, such as nonfat milk and nonfat, plain yogurt.

Combine all of the ingredients in a blender and blend on high for 1 to 2 minutes, until smooth.

 PER SERVING CALORIES: 68; PROTEIN: 2G; TOTAL FAT: 6G; SATURATED FAT: 2G; CARBOHYDRATES: 3G; SUGAR: 0G; FIBER: 0G; SODIUM: 64MG

Tropical Smoothie

Using frozen rather than fresh mango helps thicken this smoothie. Choose light canned coconut milk, which is low in fat and fiber. This smoothie will keep in the refrigerator for up to three days. You can also freeze it in single-serving ice pops to eat straight from the freezer, or run it in the blender to turn it back into a smoothie.

SERVES 6

Serving size: 4 ounces

Prep time: 5 minutes

Cook time: None

½ cup frozen mango

½ cup light coconut milk

½ cup nonfat plain coconut or almond yogurt

1 tablespoon almond butter

Substitution Tip: If you tolerate dairy well, feel free to replace the coconut milk and coconut yogurt with nonfat dairy versions. You can also add 2 tablespoons of nonfat milk powder to boost the protein.

Combine all of the ingredients in a blender and blend on high for 1 to 2 minutes, until smooth.

PER SERVING CALORIES: 87; PROTEIN: 1G; TOTAL FAT: 5G; SATURATED FAT: 3G; CARBOHYDRATES: 9G; SUGAR: 5G; FIBER: 1G; SODIUM: 12MG

Nikki's Vegan Smoothie

DAIRY-FREE | GLUTEN-FREE

Nikki Weber has suffered from gastroparesis for the past five years. We share her story in Appendix B: Stories from the Front Line starting on page 174. Her recipe calls for PB2 powder, a powdered peanut butter that you can find in health food stores or online.

SERVES 1

Serving size: 1 smoothie

Prep time: 5 minutes

Cook time: None

––––––––––

½ cup almond milk (vanilla or chocolate)

½ frozen banana

2 tablespoons PB2 powder

¼ cup ice

Substitution Tip: If you can't find PB2 powder, replace it with 1 tablespoon of peanut butter.

Combine all of the ingredients in a blender and blend until smooth.

 PER SERVING CALORIES: 158; PROTEIN: 11G; TOTAL FAT: 4G; SATURATED FAT: 0G; CARBOHYDRATES: 24G; SUGAR: 9G; FIBER: 6G; SODIUM: 279MG

Sweet Potato Pie Smoothie

GLUTEN-FREE | DAIRY-FREE

Using canned sweet potatoes makes this recipe a snap. If you like, you can also cook sweet potatoes yourself—just bake them and scoop out the flesh of the potato to make the smoothie. Feel free to adjust the spices to meet your own tastes.

SERVES 1
Serving size: 8 ounces
Prep time: 5 minutes
Cook time: None

─────────

6 ounces almond milk
¼ cup mashed canned sweet potatoes
¼ cup pure maple syrup
¼ teaspoon ground ginger
¼ teaspoon pumpkin pie spice

Substitution Tip: If you don't want sugar, you can change the maple syrup to three to four drops of liquid stevia and ⅛ teaspoon of maple flavoring.

Combine all ingredients in a blender and blend until smooth.

 PER SERVING CALORIES: 274; PROTEIN: 1G; TOTAL FAT: 2G; SATURATED FAT: 0G; CARBOHYDRATES: 65G; SUGAR: 47G; FIBER: 2G; SODIUM: 117MG

5

BREAKFAST & BRUNCH

Yogurt with Blueberry Sauce

GLUTEN-FREE

This recipe makes a delicious breakfast or a tasty quick snack. You can make the blueberry sauce in bulk, doubling or tripling the recipe and freezing it in quarter-cup servings for up to six months. Otherwise, the blueberry sauce will keep in the refrigerator for up to three days. This breakfast is high in calcium and antioxidants.

SERVES 2

Serving size: ½ cup cup yogurt,
  plus 2 tablespoons blueberry sauce
Prep time: 5 minutes, plus 1 hour to chill
Cook time: 10 minutes

———————

½ cup frozen or fresh blueberries
2 tablespoons water
1 to 2 drops liquid stevia (optional)
¼ teaspoon ground cinnamon
1 cup nonfat, plain yogurt

Substitution Tip: If you don't tolerate dairy or if you want to make this dish low in FODMAPs, replace the yogurt with a nonfat, nondairy yogurt such as plain coconut yogurt or plain almond yogurt.

1. In a small saucepan, heat the blueberries, water, stevia (if using), and cinnamon over medium-high heat until simmering, stirring frequently, about 5 minutes.

2. Pour the mixture into a blender and blend on high for 1 minute.

3. Strain the sauce through a fine-mesh strainer into a small bowl. Cover and refrigerate the sauce until it's chilled, about 1 hour.

4. To serve, spoon 2 tablespoons of the blueberry sauce over ½ cup of yogurt in each bowl.

 PER SERVING CALORIES: 81; PROTEIN: 6G; TOTAL FAT: 0G; SATURATED FAT: 0G; CARBOHYDRATES: 14G; SUGAR: 13G; FIBER: 1G; SODIUM: 90MG

Apple-Almond Cream of Rice Cereal

DAIRY-FREE | GLUTEN-FREE

It's easy to make your own rice cereal using a blender or food processor. By grinding the rice into meal, it cooks more quickly and has a porridge-like consistency. Using rice instead of wheat also makes the cereal gluten-free. To lower the sugar content, replace the pure maple syrup with stevia drops.

SERVES 6

Serving size: ½ cup
Prep time: 5 minutes
Cook time: 10 minutes

———————

1 cup uncooked white rice
2 cups apple juice
2 cups water
½ cup Rice Milk (page 56)
2 tablespoons almond butter
2 tablespoons pure maple syrup
½ teaspoon ground cinnamon
Pinch sea salt

Substitution Tip: To increase the protein content, if you tolerate dairy well, add 2 tablespoons of nonfat dry milk powder to the liquid as you bring it to a boil.

1. In a blender, add the rice and blend on high until it is coarsely chopped into meal, about 3 minutes.

2. In a small saucepan, bring the apple juice, water, rice milk, almond butter, maple syrup, cinnamon, and salt to a boil, stirring occasionally.

3. Slowly add the rice meal to the mixture, stirring constantly.

4. Reduce the heat to medium. Cover the pot and simmer for 4 to 5 minutes, until the cereal is tender. Stir before serving.

 PER SERVING CALORIES: 209; PROTEIN: 3G; TOTAL FAT: 4G; SATURATED FAT: 0G; CARBOHYDRATES: 41G; SUGAR: 13G; FIBER: 1G; SODIUM: 42MG

Banana Pancakes with Strawberry Sauce

GLUTEN-FREE | DAIRY-FREE | LOW-FODMAP | SIBO-FRIENDLY

These banana pancakes are super easy to make, nutrient dense, and grain free! When topped with a simple strawberry sauce made from fresh or frozen strawberries, they make a delicious, nutritious breakfast for the whole family.

SERVES 4

Serving size: 1 pancake and
  2 tablespoons of strawberry sauce
Prep time: 10 minutes
Cook time: 10 minutes

For the sauce

1 cup strawberries, hulled
2 tablespoons water
1 to 2 drops liquid stevia (optional)

For the pancakes

2 bananas, peeled and mashed
4 eggs, beaten
Pinch sea salt
1 tablespoon coconut oil

Substitution Tip: For a bit more protein, spread each pancake with ½ tablespoon of almond butter before adding the strawberry sauce.

To make the sauce

1. In a small saucepan, heat the strawberries, water, and stevia (if using) over medium-high heat, mashing the strawberries with a spoon as they cook.

2. Bring the mixture to a boil and cook, stirring constantly, for 4 minutes.

3. Transfer the mixture to a blender, and blend on high for 1 minute.

4. Strain the sauce through a fine-mesh sieve into a small bowl and set aside.

To make the pancakes

1. In a small bowl, whisk together the mashed bananas, eggs, and salt.

2. Heat a nonstick griddle over medium-high heat and brush it with coconut oil.

3. Spoon the batter onto the griddle using about ¼ cup per pancake. Cook for 1 to 2 minutes on each side, until golden.

4. Serve each pancake topped with 2 tablespoons of the strawberry sauce.

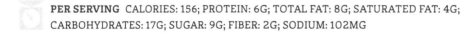 **PER SERVING** CALORIES: 156; PROTEIN: 6G; TOTAL FAT: 8G; SATURATED FAT: 4G; CARBOHYDRATES: 17G; SUGAR: 9G; FIBER: 2G; SODIUM: 102MG

Vanilla-Orange French Toast

GLUTEN-FREE | DAIRY-FREE | LOW-FODMAP | SIBO-FRIENDLY

Using gluten-free bread allows people with wheat allergies or gluten sensitivities to enjoy French toast. The trick to good French toast is soaking the bread long enough to give it a custard-like consistency. Orange zest adds a pleasant, citrusy flavor to the custard.

SERVES 6

Serving size: 1 piece

Prep time: 10 minutes

Cook time: 10 minutes

————

1 cup Almond Milk (page 57)

Zest of ½ orange

Juice of 1 orange, strained

4 eggs, beaten

1 to 2 drops liquid stevia

½ teaspoon ground cinnamon

6 slices gluten-free white bread, crusts trimmed

1 teaspoon melted coconut oil

Dash ground nutmeg

Ingredient Tip: When zesting an orange, make sure to use only the orange part of the peel and not the bitter white part (the pith). The best way to zest an orange is to use a rasp-style grater and carefully remove the orange peel's top surface.

1. In a small bowl, whisk together the almond milk, zest, juice, eggs, stevia, and cinnamon. Pour the mixture into a shallow dish.

2. Soak the bread in the custard mixture for about 3 minutes on each side.

3. While the bread soaks, heat a large nonstick skillet to medium-high. Brush the skillet with the melted coconut oil.

4. Put the custard-soaked bread on the griddle, sprinkling each slice with nutmeg.

5. Cook until the custard sets, about 4 minutes per side.

 PER SERVING CALORIES: 170; PROTEIN: 6G; TOTAL FAT: 6G; SATURATED FAT: 2G; CARBOHYDRATES: 24G; SUGAR: 7G; FIBER: 2G; SODIUM: 217MG

Mushroom and Thyme Scrambled Eggs

GLUTEN-FREE | DAIRY-FREE | LOW-CARB | LOW-SUGAR | GERD-FRIENDLY

Thyme perfectly complements the earthy mushrooms in this simple scrambled egg dish. You can use any type of fresh mushrooms, although chanterelles are especially delicious in this dish. Unused portions can be stored in the refrigerator for up to three days and reheated in the microwave.

SERVES 6
Serving size: ½ cup
Prep time: 10 minutes
Cook time: 10 minutes

———————

2 tablespoons extra-virgin olive oil
2 cups sliced mushrooms
½ teaspoon sea salt
6 eggs, beaten
1 teaspoon dried thyme

Ingredient Tip: To clean mushrooms, wipe them gently with a damp paper towel or use a soft mushroom brush. Do not submerge the mushrooms in water, because they act as sponges and will soak it up.

1. In a large, nonstick skillet, heat the olive oil over medium-high heat until shimmering.

2. Add the mushrooms. Let them sit in the hot skillet for 3 minutes before stirring them.

3. Sprinkle the mushrooms with the salt. Continue cooking, stirring occasionally, until all the liquid has evaporated and the mushrooms are browned, about 4 minutes.

4. In a small bowl, whisk together the eggs and thyme.

5. Pour the egg mixture over the mushrooms in the skillet and cook, stirring occasionally, until the eggs set, another 2 to 3 minutes.

 PER SERVING CALORIES: 108; PROTEIN: 3G; TOTAL FAT: 9G; SATURATED FAT: 2G; CARBOHYDRATES: 1G; SUGAR: 1G; FIBER: 0G; SODIUM: 257MG

Shrimp and Spinach Frittata

GLUTEN-FREE | LOW-CARB | LOW-SUGAR

This egg dish is high in protein, low in fat, and really tasty. It also has plenty of vitamins and minerals from the spinach, making it a healthy and low-carbohydrate way to start your morning. To make the frittata dairy free, eliminate the Parmesan cheese. You can also save the leftover frittata in the refrigerator for up to three days, reheating it in the microwave for additional breakfasts or lunches.

SERVES 6

Serving size: ⅙ of the frittata
Prep time: 10 minutes
Cook time: 15 minutes

———————

2 tablespoons extra-virgin olive oil
2 cups baby spinach, stems trimmed
4 ounces cooked baby shrimp
Pinch ground nutmeg
4 whole eggs
4 egg whites
½ teaspoon dried tarragon
½ teaspoon sea salt
¼ cup low-fat grated Parmesan cheese

Substitution Tip: Tarragon goes quite well with seafood, and many people love its delicate flavor. If you can find fresh tarragon, it will be even more flavorful. To use fresh tarragon in place of dried in this recipe, use about 1 teaspoon of the chopped, fresh herb.

1. Preheat the broiler.

2. In a 12-inch ovenproof skillet, heat the olive oil over medium-high heat until it shimmers. Add the spinach and cook, stirring frequently, for 2 minutes.

3. Add the shrimp and nutmeg and cook for 2 more minutes.

4. In a small bowl, whisk together the eggs, egg whites, tarragon, and salt.

5. Carefully pour the mixture over the spinach and shrimp in the skillet. Cook for 2 to 3 minutes without stirring until the eggs solidify around the edges.

6. Using a rubber spatula, carefully pull the cooked eggs away from the edges of the pan. Tilt the pan to allow uncooked eggs to run into the gaps. Cook for another minute.

7. Sprinkle with the Parmesan cheese. Place the skillet under the broiler. Cook for 2 to 3 minutes, until the frittata puffs and browns and the cheese melts.

PER SERVING CALORIES: 126; PROTEIN: 11G; TOTAL FAT: 9G; SATURATED FAT: 2G; CARBOHYDRATES: 1G; SUGAR: 1G; FIBER: 0G; SODIUM: 441MG

Poached Eggs over Sweet Potato Hash

GLUTEN-FREE | DAIRY-FREE | LOW-FODMAP | LOW-SUGAR
SIBO-FRIENDLY | GERD-FRIENDLY

Sweet potatoes are high in vitamins A and C, and they have a delicious earthy flavor that works well with poached eggs. Putting the egg on top of the hash allows the yolk to run into the hash, giving it wonderful flavor.

SERVES 4
Serving size: 1 egg and ¼ cup hash
Prep time: 10 minutes
Cook time: 15 minutes

———

1 sweet potato, peeled and patted dry
2 tablespoons extra-virgin olive oil
½ teaspoon sea salt
4 eggs

Cooking Tip: To make poaching eggs easier, crack each egg into a custard cup and then hold the custard cup directly above the barely simmering water and gently slip it in.

1. Cut the sweet potato into ½-inch cubes.

2. In a large nonstick skillet over medium-high heat, heat the olive oil until it shimmers.

3. Add the sweet potato and cook without stirring for 5 minutes.

4. Add the salt and continue cooking, stirring occasionally, until the sweet potatoes are browned, about 5 more minutes.

5. While the sweet potato cooks, bring a medium pot of water to a simmer.

6. Carefully crack open the eggs and gently slip the whole yolk with attached egg white into the water. Poach for about 4 minutes.

7. While the eggs are poaching, divide the hash onto 4 plates.

8. Remove the poached eggs from the water with a slotted spoon, and place each egg atop a mound of the hash.

PER SERVING CALORIES: 149; PROTEIN: 6G; TOTAL FAT: 11G; SATURATED FAT: 2G; CARBOHYDRATES: 6G; SUGAR: 2G; FIBER: 1G; SODIUM: 306MG

Avocado and Herb Omelet

GLUTEN-FREE | LOW-FODMAP | LOW-CARB | LOW-SUGAR
SIBO-FRIENDLY | GERD-FRIENDLY

Herbs can make an omelet extremely flavorful. Fresh herbs work best in this omelet, although if necessary you can substitute dried herbs using half the amount required for fresh herbs. Avocados are full of nutrition, giving you plenty of energy and lots of nutrients, including vitamin E and potassium.

SERVES 3
Serving size: ⅓ omelet
Prep time: 5 minutes
Cook time: 10 minutes

———————

¼ cup low-fat cream cheese
1 teaspoon chopped fresh tarragon
1 teaspoon chopped fresh thyme
1 teaspoon chopped fresh fennel fronds
1 tablespoon extra-virgin olive oil
2 whole eggs
3 egg whites
½ teaspoon sea salt
¼ avocado, thinly sliced

Ingredient Tip: To select an avocado, choose a fruit that yields slightly to light pressure from your thumb. You can also use your thumb to flick out the stem of the avocado. The stem should dislodge without much effort and the flesh underneath should be green.

1. In a small bowl, mix the cream cheese, tarragon, thyme, and fennel until well combined. Set aside.

2. In another small bowl, whisk together the eggs, egg whites, and salt.

3. In an 8-inch nonstick skillet over medium-high heat, heat the olive oil until it shimmers. Add the egg mixture and cook for 3 to 4 minutes without stirring, until the eggs begin to solidify around the edges.

4. Using a rubber spatula, carefully pull the solidified eggs away from the edge of the pan. Tilt the pan to allow the uncooked eggs to run into the spaces you created.

5. Continue cooking for another 3 to 4 minutes until the eggs have solidified on top.

6. Add the cream cheese mixture, spreading it over half of the omelet.

7. Top the cream cheese with the avocado slices.

8. Carefully fold over the omelet and allow it to cook for 1 to 2 minutes, until the cream cheese warms and melts. Serve immediately.

 **PER SERVING** CALORIES: 202; PROTEIN: 9G; TOTAL FAT: 18G; SATURATED FAT: 7G; CARBOHYDRATES: 3G; SUGAR: 1G; FIBER: 1G; SODIUM: 445MG

Acorn Squash and Egg Bake

GLUTEN-FREE | DAIRY-FREE | LOW-FODMAP | LOW-CARB
LOW-SUGAR | SIBO-FRIENDLY | GERD-FRIENDLY

This is a variation on toads in the hole, using healthy acorn squash in place of the traditional bread. Acorn squash is nutrient dense, containing healthy amounts of vitamin A, vitamin C, and magnesium. The dish is also relatively low in carbohydrates, so it makes a good breakfast for someone seeking better blood sugar control.

SERVES 4
Serving size: 1 piece
Prep time: 10 minutes
Cook time: 22 minutes

½ acorn squash, peeled, seeded and cut
    into 4 thin rings (discard the end)
2 tablespoons extra-virgin olive oil
½ teaspoon sea salt
1 teaspoon chopped fresh thyme
4 eggs

Substitution Tip: Butternut squash will also work well for this recipe. Just use slices that are about ½-inch thick.

1. Preheat the oven to 425°F. Line a baking sheet with parchment.

2. Brush each piece of squash on both sides with olive oil, and then sprinkle them with salt and thyme.

3. Bake in the preheated oven for 10 minutes, until the squash is tender.

4. Remove from the oven and crack 1 egg into the center hole of each piece of squash. Sprinkle the eggs with a little salt.

5. Return to the oven and continue cooking for 10 to 12 minutes until the eggs are set and cooked.

 PER SERVING CALORIES: 145; PROTEIN: 6G; TOTAL FAT: 11G; SATURATED FAT: 2G; CARBOHYDRATES: 6G; SUGAR: 0G; FIBER: 1G; SODIUM: 122MG

Turkey Breakfast Sausage

GLUTEN-FREE | DAIRY-FREE | LOW-FODMAP | LOW-CARB
LOW-SUGAR | SIBO-FRIENDLY | GERD-FRIENDLY

You can make patties out of this turkey breakfast sausage, or cook it crumbled and add it to scrambled eggs or an omelet. Choose extra-lean turkey made from skinless turkey breast. It will add a mild but flavorful pop of protein to any breakfast.

SERVES 4
Serving size: 2 ounces
Prep time: 5 minutes
Cook time: 10 minutes

———

8 ounces ground turkey breast
½ teaspoon sea salt
½ teaspoon ground sage
½ teaspoon dried thyme
1 tablespoon extra-virgin olive oil

Substitution Tip: If you like the flavor of maple in your breakfast sausage and you don't have problems with blood sugar control, add 2 table-spoons of pure maple syrup to the sausage mixture.

1. In a medium bowl, mix together the turkey breast, salt, sage, and thyme.

2. In a medium nonstick skillet, heat the olive oil over medium-high heat until it shimmers.

3. Form the sausage into 4 patties and cook, browning on both sides, about 4 minutes per side.

4. Serve hot.

 PER SERVING CALORIES: 138; PROTEIN: 16G; TOTAL FAT: 7G; SATURATED FAT: 2G; CARBOHYDRATES: 0G; SUGAR: 0G; FIBER: 0G; SODIUM: 270MG

6

SNACKS, SIDES & APPETIZERS

Cheesy Mashed Potatoes

GLUTEN-FREE | GERD-FRIENDLY

Make a classic comfort food even tastier by adding delicious cheese and herbs. This is a great side dish for virtually any meal, or you can have it alone as a tasty snack. Potatoes are quite starchy, so they may not be appropriate for people with blood sugar control issues. The potatoes will keep, refrigerated, for up to three days. They also freeze well.

SERVES 4

Serving size: ¼ cup
Prep time: 10 minutes
Cook time: 15 minutes

———————

2 medium russet potatoes,
    peeled and cut into 1-inch pieces
¼ cup nonfat milk
¼ cup nonfat cream cheese
¼ cup grated low-fat Cheddar cheese
½ teaspoon chopped fresh thyme
¼ teaspoon chopped, fresh rosemary
½ teaspoon sea salt

Substitution Tip: Any type of peeled potatoes will work in this recipe. You can also substitute other root vegetables to make a lower-carbohydrate side dish, such as celeriac, turnips, carrots, or radishes depending on the types of foods you tolerate.

1. In a large pot, cover the potatoes with water. Cover and bring to a boil over medium-high heat.

2. Continue boiling until the potatoes are soft, about 10 minutes.

3. Remove the potatoes from the heat, drain them in a colander, and then return them to the hot pan.

4. Using a potato masher, mash the potatoes with the milk, cream cheese, Cheddar cheese, thyme, rosemary, and salt.

5. Serve hot.

PER SERVING CALORIES: 159; PROTEIN: 5G; TOTAL FAT: 8G; SATURATED FAT: 5G; CARBOHYDRATES: 18G; SUGAR: 2G; FIBER: 3G; SODIUM: 335MG

Root Vegetable Purée

GLUTEN-FREE | LOW-FODMAP | LOW-CARB | LOW-SUGAR
SIBO-FRIENDLY | GERD-FRIENDLY

Root vegetables have a lovely, earthy flavor that goes well with fresh thyme. By adding different types of vegetables to the purée, you expand the vitamins and minerals available in this dish. Feel free to substitute based on root vegetables you have available. This recipe will freeze well, or it will keep in the refrigerator for up to three days.

SERVES 4

Serving size: ¼ cup
Prep time: 5 minutes
Cook time: 15 minutes

———————

- 4 carrots, peeled and cut into ½-inch pieces
- 1 parsnip, peeled and cut into ½-inch pieces
- ½ rutabaga, peeled and cut into ½-inch pieces
- 1 turnip, peeled and cut into ½-inch pieces
- ½ teaspoon sea salt
- 2 tablespoons unsalted butter
- 1 teaspoon chopped fresh thyme

Cooking Tip: When blending very hot foods, it's important to allow the steam to escape through the top of the blender as you blend. To do this, remove the knob on the blender lid to allow the steam to vent, place a folded towel over the top of the blender, and put your hand on it to gently hold the lid in place.

1. In a large pot, cover the carrots, parsnips, rutabagas, and turnips with water. Cover the pot and bring to a boil over medium-high heat.

2. Cook until the vegetables are soft, about 10 minutes.

3. Drain the vegetables in a colander and transfer them to a blender.

4. Add the salt, butter, and thyme. Blend until the vegetables are smooth, about 1 minute.

 PER SERVING CALORIES: 127; PROTEIN: 2G; TOTAL FAT: 6G; SATURATED FAT: 4G; CARBOHYDRATES: 18G; SUGAR: 9G; FIBER: 5G; SODIUM: 350MG

Sweet Potato Fries

GLUTEN-FREE | DAIRY-FREE | LOW-FODMAP | SIBO-FRIENDLY | GERD-FRIENDLY

These fries make a delicious snack or side dish. They don't keep and reheat well, so it's best to make a batch at a time and eat them hot out of the oven. While the fries will be slightly crispy on the outside, on the inside they will be soft and pillowy, with a mildly sweet, earthy flavor.

SERVES 4

Serving size: ¼ sweet potato

Prep time: 10 minutes

Cook time: 30 minutes

---

1 sweet potato, peeled and patted dry

1 tablespoon extra-virgin olive oil

¼ teaspoon ground cumin

½ teaspoon sea salt

Substitution Tip: You can give the fries a slightly sweet flavor by substituting an equal amount of cinnamon for the cumin.

1. Preheat the oven to 450°F. Line a baking sheet with parchment.

2. Cut the sweet potato into ¼-inch strips and put them in a bowl.

3. Toss the strips with the olive oil, cumin, and salt.

4. Spread in a single layer on the prepared baking sheet. Bake in the preheated oven for about 30 minutes, turning the fries once or twice. The fries are done when they are golden brown and fork tender. Serve immediately.

 PER SERVING CALORIES: 56; PROTEIN: 1G; TOTAL FAT: 4G; SATURATED FAT: 1G; CARBOHYDRATES: 6G; SUGAR: 2G; FIBER: 1G; SODIUM: 244MG

Winter Squash–Ginger Spread

GLUTEN-FREE | LOW-FODMAP | SIBO-FRIENDLY | GERD-FRIENDLY

Try this spread on crackers or a piece of bread, or use it as a dip for the Sweet Potato Fries (page 82). The recipe freezes well, so you can store it in small batches to thaw whenever you're in the mood for a tasty spread. This recipe is high in vitamins A, C, and B_6, as well as magnesium and calcium.

SERVES ABOUT 6
Serving size: 2 tablespoons
Prep time: 5 minutes, plus an hour
   for the squash to cool
Cook time: 10 minutes

———————

½ butternut squash
1 tablespoon extra-virgin olive oil
½ teaspoon sea salt
½ cup nonfat plain yogurt
2 tablespoons almond butter
½ teaspoon ground ginger
¼ teaspoon ground nutmeg

Substitution Tip: For a dairy-free version, replace the yogurt with a nondairy yogurt such as coconut or almond yogurt.

1. Preheat the oven to 350°F. Line a baking sheet with parchment.

2. Brush the butternut squash with the olive oil and bake it, cut side up, on the prepared baking sheet until it is soft, about 30 minutes. Cool completely.

3. When the squash has cooled, remove the peel. Put the flesh in a blender, along with the salt, yogurt, almond butter, ginger, and nutmeg.

4. Blend until combined, about 1 minute.

5. Serve chilled.

 PER SERVING CALORIES: 110; PROTEIN: 3G; TOTAL FAT: 6G; SATURATED FAT: 1G; CARBOHYDRATES: 13G; SUGAR: 4G; FIBER: 4G; SODIUM: 174MG

Mushroom Cracker Spread

GLUTEN-FREE | LOW-CARB | LOW-SUGAR

This simple spread has the texture of a terrine or pâté, spreading easily on crackers or bread. It stores well, and can be kept in the freezer for up to six months or refrigerated for up to three days. It also makes a delicious filling for omelets, or a tasty topping for a piece of poultry or fish.

SERVES 4

Serving size: 2 tablespoons
Prep time: 5 minutes
Cook time: 15 minutes

———

2 tablespoons unsalted butter
1 cup finely chopped mushrooms
½ teaspoon dried thyme
½ teaspoon sea salt
½ cup Poultry Stock (page 147)
½ cup nonfat cream cheese

Substitution Tip: For a sharper, more herbaceous flavor, replace the thyme with 2 teaspoons of chopped, fresh rosemary.

1. In a large sauté pan, heat the butter over medium-high heat until it shimmers.

2. Add the mushrooms, thyme, and salt. Do not stir the mushroom until they have released their liquid and it has evaporated, about 5 minutes.

3. Continue cooking, stirring occasionally, until the mushrooms are deeply browned, about 5 more minutes.

4. Add the stock and cook for 2 minutes, scraping up any browned bits from the bottom of the pan with the side of the spoon.

5. Pour the mixture into a blender or food processor and add the cream cheese. Blend until smooth, about 1 minute. Serve immediately or refrigerate until ready to use.

 PER SERVING CALORIES: 159; PROTEIN: 3G; TOTAL FAT: 16G; SATURATED FAT: 10G; CARBOHYDRATES: 2G; SUGAR: 0G; FIBER: 0G; SODIUM: 378MG

Cream Cheese and Herb Spread

GLUTEN-FREE | LOW-FODMAP | LOW-CARB

This is another spread that goes well on bread or crackers. It also makes a delicious, low-carbohydrate topping for fish or poultry. Feel free to substitute any herbs that are in season to lend this cream cheese spread a delicious, seasonal flavor.

SERVES 6

Serving size: 2 tablespoons

Prep time: 5 minutes

Cook time: None

¾ cup nonfat cream cheese,
    at room temperature

1 tablespoon chopped fresh dill

1 tablespoon chopped fresh basil

1 teaspoon chopped, fresh thyme

½ teaspoon sea salt

½ teaspoon lemon zest

Substitution Tip: You can substitute any low-fat soft cheese in this recipe, such as Neufchatel cheese or a soft, low-fat goat cheese.

In a small bowl, combine all of the ingredients and mix well. Serve at room temperature or chill before serving.

 PER SERVING CALORIES: 33; PROTEIN: 4G; TOTAL FAT: 0G; SATURATED FAT: 0G; CARBOHYDRATES: 3G; SUGAR: 2G; FIBER: 0G; SODIUM: 357MG

Creamed Spinach

GLUTEN-FREE | DAIRY-FREE | LOW-FODMAP | LOW-CARB
LOW-SUGAR | SIBO-FRIENDLY | GERD-FRIENDLY

Spinach is a nutritional powerhouse, containing antioxidants, iron, vitamin A, vitamin C, and magnesium. In this side dish, the flavor of nutmeg complements the flavors in spinach surprisingly well, which is why it's added here.

SERVES 4
Serving size: ¼ cup
Prep time: 5 minutes
Cook time: 15 minutes

---

2 tablespoons extra-virgin olive oil
1 pound baby spinach, trimmed
¼ cup Almond Milk (page 57)
¼ teaspoon orange zest
½ teaspoon ground nutmeg
½ teaspoon sea salt

Ingredient Tip: Remove any fibrous stems from the spinach before you cook it, cutting them away with a sharp knife and discarding.

1. In a large sauté pan over medium-high heat, heat the olive oil until it shimmers.

2. Add the spinach in two or three batches, adding more as each batch wilts. Cook for 3 or 4 minutes, stirring frequently, until all liquid evaporate.

3. Add the almond milk, zest, nutmeg, and salt.

4. Cook, stirring frequently, until the sauce thickens slightly, about 10 minutes.

PER SERVING CALORIES: 96; PROTEIN: 4G; TOTAL FAT: 8G; SATURATED FAT: 1G; CARBOHYDRATES: 5G; SUGAR: 1G; FIBER: 3G; SODIUM: 324MG

Orange-Cranberry Gelatin

GLUTEN-FREE | DAIRY-FREE | LOW-FODMAP | SIBO-FRIENDLY | GERD-FRIENDLY

The gentle sweetness of the oranges blend well with the tartness of the cranberries. You can eat this gelatin as a snack, or use it as a side dish for turkey or chicken. It keeps in the refrigerator for up to three days.

SERVES ABOUT 12

Serving size: ¼ cup
Prep time: 15 minutes,
    plus overnight to chill
Cook time: None

———

⅓ cup cranberry juice
½ cup orange juice, strained
1 cup cold water
2 tablespoons gelatin
1½ cups hot water
1 to 2 drops liquid stevia (optional)

Ingredient Tip: Try to find gelatin made from organic, pastured animals. My favorite brand is Great Lakes unflavored gelatin, which you can find online or at many health food stores.

1. In a medium bowl, combine the cranberry juice, orange juice, and cold water.

2. Whisk in the gelatin slowly, until it completely dissolves.

3. Add the hot water and stevia (if using), stirring to combine.

4. Cover the gelatin mixture and refrigerate overnight to set.

 PER SERVING CALORIES: 10; PROTEIN: 1G; TOTAL FAT: 0G; SATURATED FAT: 0G; CARBOHYDRATES: 1G; SUGAR: 1G; FIBER: 0G; SODIUM: 2MG

Summer Squash and Lemon Dip or Spread

GLUTEN-FREE | DAIRY-FREE | LOW-SUGAR | LOW-CARB

Unfortunately, for many people with gastroparesis, hummus is no longer on the menu because it contains chickpeas. This lemony spread incorporates some of the flavors of hummus without the fibrous chickpeas. Instead, it relies on cooked summer squash as its base flavored with lemon zest, and herbaceous Italian parsley. Use it as a spread or a dip for crackers.

SERVES ABOUT 8

Serving size: 2 tablespoons

Prep time: 10 minutes, plus 1 hour
   for squash to cool

Cook time: 10 minutes

———

2 tablespoons extra-virgin
   olive oil, divided

2 cups peeled, cubed summer squash

½ teaspoon sea salt

1 tablespoon tahini

Zest of ½ lemon

Juice of ½ lemon, strained

¼ teaspoon ground cumin

Substitution Tip: If tahini causes issues, you can replace it with a tablespoon of almond butter, or omit it altogether.

1. In a large nonstick sauté pan over medium-high heat, heat 1 tablespoon olive oil until it shimmers. Add the summer squash and cook, stirring occasionally, until it is soft, about 5 minutes.

2. Allow the squash to cool completely, about 1 hour.

3. Transfer the cooled squash to a blender or food processor. Add the remaining 1 tablespoon of olive oil, the salt, tahini, zest, juice, and cumin.

4. Blend until smooth, about 1 minute. Serve immediately or chill before serving.

PER SERVING CALORIES: 61; PROTEIN: 1G; TOTAL FAT: 6G; SATURATED FAT: 1G; CARBOHYDRATES: 1G; SUGAR: 1G; FIBER: 0G; SODIUM: 120MG

Maple–Butternut Squash Purée

GLUTEN-FREE

Maple syrup brings warmth and sweetness to earthy butternut squash while a tiny bit of orange zest adds additional flavor. The result is a vibrantly flavored purée that makes a delicious side dish for poultry or fish, or works as a tasty snack. It will keep in the refrigerator for up to three days.

SERVES ABOUT 8
Serving size: ¼ cup
Prep time: 10 minutes
Cook time: 40 minutes

---

1 pound butternut squash, halved
    with pulp and seeds removed
2 tablespoons extra-virgin olive oil
½ teaspoon sea salt
Zest of ½ orange
3 tablespoons pure maple syrup
½ teaspoon ground cinnamon

Ingredient Tip: Extra virgin olive oil (EVOO) is a flavorful and healthy fat. Unfortunately, many brands of olive oil aren't made with pure extra-virgin olive oil, but may contain canola or other oils. One way to tell whether your brand is EVOO is to refrigerate a small amount. If it solidifies in the refrigerator, it is likely EVOO.

1. Preheat the oven to 350°F. Brush the cut sides of the squash with olive oil and place them skin-side down on a baking sheet.

2. Roast in the preheated oven for 30 to 40 minutes until tender.

3. Use a spoon to scoop the squash flesh away from the rind. Put the flesh in a blender.

4. Add the salt, zest, maple syrup, and cinnamon. Blend the mixture until smooth. Serve immediately.

 PER SERVING CALORIES: 76; PROTEIN: 1G; TOTAL FAT: 4G; SATURATED FAT: 1G; CARBOHYDRATES: 12G; SUGAR: 6G; FIBER: 1G; SODIUM: 120MG

7
SOUPS & STEWS

Creamy Tomato-Basil Soup

GLUTEN-FREE | DAIRY-FREE | LOW-CARB | LOW-SUGAR

Tomatoes and basil are a classic flavor combination. The minty bite of the basil complements the sweet acidity of tomatoes. This recipe calls for use of any strained tomato or vegetable juice (such as V8), but if you have a juicer you can make your own base instead.

SERVES 6
Serving size: ½ cup
Prep time: 5 minutes
Cook time: 15 minutes

---

1 tablespoon extra-virgin olive oil
3 scallions, green parts only, chopped
3 large carrots, peeled and chopped
2 cups tomato juice, strained
½ teaspoon sea salt
¾ cup Almond Milk (page 57)
2 tablespoons chopped fresh basil

Substitution Tip: The purpose of the carrots is to add a little bit of sweetness and to give the soup some body without relying on thickeners such as flour. You can replace the carrot with sweet potato or another root vegetable such as turnips if you wish.

1. In a medium pot, heat the olive oil over medium-high heat until it shimmers. Add the scallions and carrots and cook, stirring frequently, until vegetables soften, about 5 minutes.

2. Add the tomato juice and salt and bring the mixture to a simmer. Reduce the heat to medium and continue to simmer until the carrots are very soft, about 10 minutes.

3. Transfer the mixture to a blender. Add the almond milk and basil.

4. Blend on high until smooth, about 1 minute. Serve immediately.

 PER SERVING CALORIES: 57; PROTEIN: 1G; TOTAL FAT: 3G; SATURATED FAT: 0G; CARBOHYDRATES: 7G; SUGAR: 4G; FIBER: 2G; SODIUM: 400MG

Tomato and Vegetable Soup

GLUTEN-FREE | DAIRY-FREE | LOW-CARB | LOW-SUGAR

In this soup, tomatoes combine with other well-cooked vegetables to provide plenty of vitamins, minerals, and antioxidants. This soup keeps well, so you can make a large batch and freeze it for up to six months. Store in individual serving sizes to make it easy to thaw for a meal on the go.

SERVES 6
Serving size: ½ cup
Prep time: 10 minutes
Cook time: 30 minutes

———————

2 tablespoons extra-virgin olive oil

3 scallions, green parts only, chopped

4 pieces roasted red pepper
(from a jar), chopped

1 carrot, peeled and chopped

1 medium summer squash,
peeled and chopped

1 cup baby spinach, stems removed

1 cup Poultry Stock (page 147)

1½ cups tomato juice, strained

½ teaspoon ground cumin

¼ teaspoon orange zest

½ teaspoon sea salt

Substitution Tip: This recipe works really well as a "dump soup," where you can add any vegetables you may have available. Consider adding zucchini, butternut squash, mushrooms, sweet potatoes, or any other vegetables you enjoy.

1. In a medium pot, heat the olive oil over medium-high heat until it shimmers.

2. Add the scallions, roasted red pepper, carrot, and summer squash. Cook, stirring occasionally, until vegetables soften, about 5 minutes.

3. Add the spinach and cook, stirring occasionally, until the spinach wilts, about 1 minute more.

4. Add the stock, tomato juice, cumin, zest, and salt. Bring the pot to a simmer. Reduce the heat to medium-low and continue to simmer the soup until the vegetables are very soft, about 10 minutes more.

5. Cook, stirring frequently, until the sauce thickens slightly, about 10 minutes.

 PER SERVING CALORIES: 69; PROTEIN: 2G; TOTAL FAT: 5G; SATURATED FAT: 1G; CARBOHYDRATES: 5G; SUGAR: 4G; FIBER: 1G; SODIUM: 329MG

Roasted Root Vegetable Soup

GLUTEN-FREE | DAIRY-FREE | LOW-FODMAP | SIBO-FRIENDLY | GERD-FRIENDLY

You can try this soup two ways: as a clear soup with bits of vegetables floating in it, or as a puréed, thicker soup. Root vegetables have plenty of starch, and when puréed, can give the soup a thick, creamy texture without dairy products. Roasting the vegetables adds a caramelized sweetness to the soup.

SERVES 8

Serving size: ½ cup
Prep time: 10 minutes
Cook time: 45 minutes

———————

1 sweet potato, peeled and cut into
    ½-inch pieces
1 carrot, peeled and chopped into
    ½-inch pieces
1 parsnip, peeled and chopped into
    ½-inch pieces
1 tablespoon extra-virgin olive oil
½ teaspoon sea salt
1 teaspoon dried thyme
3 cups Vegetable Stock (page 145)

Substitution Tip: If sweet potatoes bother you, you can replace them with butternut squash. You can also replace the parsnips with turnips or more carrots, depending on your taste and tolerances.

1. Preheat the oven to 425°F. In a large ovenproof Dutch oven or pot, toss the sweet potato, carrot, and parsnip with the olive oil, salt, and thyme.

2. Roast the vegetables in the preheated oven for 25 to 30 minutes, or until the vegetables are tender.

3. Remove the pot from the oven and place it on the stove. Add the vegetable stock and bring to a simmer over medium-high heat. As the soup heats, scrape any browned bits from the bottom of the pan with the side of a wooden spoon.

4. Simmer for 10 minutes.

5. If you prefer a chunky vegetable soup, serve as is. Otherwise, purée the soup in a blender. Serve immediately or return to the pot and reheat before serving if necessary.

 PER SERVING CALORIES: 49; PROTEIN: 1G; TOTAL FAT: 2G; SATURATED FAT: 0G; CARBOHYDRATES: 8G; SUGAR: 3G; FIBER: 2G; SODIUM: 343MG

Butternut Squash Soup

GLUTEN-FREE | DAIRY-FREE | LOW-FODMAP | SIBO-FRIENDLY | GERD-FRIENDLY

This simple soup is hearty and delicious, and it makes a warming meal in the fall. Fresh tarragon adds a delicate, distinctive flavor to the soup. Other fresh herbs, such as thyme or chopped rosemary, will work well in place of tarragon if it's not available. This soup freezes well.

SERVES 8

Serving size: ½ cup
Prep time: 10 minutes
Cook time: 20 minutes

———

3 cups Vegetable Stock (page 145)
1½ cups butternut squash, peeled, pulp removed, and cut into 1-inch pieces
½ teaspoon sea salt
½ teaspoon ground cinnamon
¼ teaspoon orange zest
2 tablespoons chopped fresh tarragon

Ingredient Tip: Many grocery stores now offer cubed butternut squash in packages, either fresh or frozen. To save time, you can use this pre-cut, pre-peeled squash.

1. In a large pot, combine the stock, butternut squash, salt, cinnamon, and zest.

2. Bring the soup to a simmer over medium-high heat, stirring occasionally, until the squash is soft, about 15 minutes.

3. Transfer the soup to a blender and add the tarragon. Blend until smooth, about 1 minute.

4. Return the soup to the pot and reheat if needed. Serve immediately.

PER SERVING CALORIES: 18; PROTEIN: 1G; TOTAL FAT: 0G; SATURATED FAT: 0G; CARBOHYDRATES: 4G; SUGAR: 1G; FIBER: 1G; SODIUM: 156MG

Carrot-Ginger Soup

GLUTEN-FREE | DAIRY-FREE | LOW-FODMAP | SIBO-FRIENDLY | GERD-FRIENDLY

This classic flavor combination makes a tasty, satisfying soup. Try it with some of the heirloom carrots that are available in colors like red, purple, and white for a more interesting presentation. While the recipe calls for puréeing, you can also leave the soup with chunks of vegetables if you prefer.

SERVES 8

Serving size: ½ cup

Prep time: 10 minutes

Cook time: 20 minutes

---

1 tablespoon extra-virgin olive oil

1 tablespoon grated peeled fresh ginger

3 scallions, green parts only, chopped

3½ cups Vegetable Stock (page 145) or Poultry Stock (page 147)

6 large carrots, peeled and cut into ½-inch pieces

Pinch nutmeg

½ teaspoon sea salt

Substitution Tip: Try making this tasty soup with sweet potato or winter squash in place of the carrots for an interesting variation.

1. In a large pot, heat the olive oil over medium-high heat until it shimmers.

2. Add the ginger and scallion and cook, stirring occasionally, until fragrant, about 2 minutes.

3. Add the stock, carrots, nutmeg, and salt. Bring the stock to a simmer. Reduce the heat to medium-low and continue to simmer the soup, stirring occasionally, until the carrots are soft, about 15 minutes.

4. Transfer the hot liquid to a blender and blend on high until puréed, about 1 minute.

5. Serve immediately or return to the pot to reheat before serving if needed.

 PER SERVING CALORIES: 46; PROTEIN: 1G; TOTAL FAT: 2G; SATURATED FAT: 0G; CARBOHYDRATES: 7G; SUGAR: 3G; FIBER: 2G; SODIUM: 345MG

Turkey-Ginger Soup

GLUTEN-FREE | DAIRY-FREE | LOW-FODMAP | LOW-CARB
LOW-SUGAR | SIBO-FRIENDLY | GERD-FRIENDLY

Ground turkey adds protein to this soup, while vegetables add additional nutrients. To save time, you can use frozen vegetables in place of fresh. This soup freezes exceptionally well, and it's simple enough to make a double or triple batch to stock in your freezer.

SERVES 10
Serving size: ½ cup
Prep time: 10 minutes
Cook time: 30 minutes

———

1 tablespoon extra-virgin olive oil
3 scallions, green parts only,
    chopped (optional)
2 tablespoons grated peeled fresh ginger
1 pound ground turkey
4 cups Poultry Stock (page 147)
2 carrots, peeled and diced
1 crookneck squash, peeled and diced
½ teaspoon sea salt
½ teaspoon ground turmeric

Ingredient Tip: Choose ground turkey made from skinless turkey breast to keep protein content high and fat low.

1. In a large pot, heat the olive oil over medium-high heat until it shimmers.

2. Add the scallions (if using) and ginger. Sauté, stirring constantly, for 1 minute.

3. Add the ground turkey to the pot, breaking the meat apart with the side of your spoon until it's cooked through, about 5 minutes.

4. Add the stock, carrots, squash, salt, and turmeric and bring the soup to a simmer.

5. Reduce the heat to medium-low and continue to simmer the soup until the vegetables are very soft, 15 to 20 minutes.

6. Serve hot.

PER SERVING CALORIES: 125; PROTEIN: 15G; TOTAL FAT: 7G; SATURATED FAT: 1G; CARBOHYDRATES: 4G; SUGAR: 2G; FIBER: 1G; SODIUM: 204MG

Chicken Noodle Soup

DAIRY-FREE | GERD-FRIENDLY

With plenty of healthy veggies and protein from the chicken, this classic soup is a wonderful all-purpose meal. Serve it for lunch or dinner, or take it with you for a work lunch. Whenever you choose to eat it, chicken soup is a warm and satisfying meal. This soup freezes well.

SERVES 10
Serving size: ½ cup
Prep time: 10 minutes
Cook time: 30 minutes

―――――

1 tablespoon extra-virgin olive oil

3 scallions, green parts only, chopped

10 ounces chicken breast, cut into
    ½-inch pieces

4 cups Poultry Stock (page 147)

3 carrots, peeled and chopped

½ teaspoon lemon zest

2 ounces spaghetti noodles

½ teaspoon sea salt

Substitution Tip: To make this soup gluten-free and low-carb, substitute "zoodles" (zucchini noodles) for the spaghetti. To make zoodles, use a spiralizer or an apple peeler (or a vegetable peeler will do) to remove long strips of peeled zucchini and then cut the strips into noodle shapes with a knife.

1. In a large pot, heat the olive oil over medium-high heat until it shimmers.

2. Add the scallions and chicken breast and cook, stirring occasionally, until the chicken meat is cooked, about 5 minutes.

3. Add the stock, carrots, and zest. Bring to a boil and reduce the heat to medium. Simmer, stirring occasionally, until the carrots are soft, about 10 minutes.

4. Add the spaghetti and salt, then raise the heat to medium-high and bring to a boil. Boil for 8 to 10 minutes until the noodles are soft. Serve hot.

PER SERVING CALORIES: 92; PROTEIN: 12G; TOTAL FAT: 3G; SATURATED FAT: 0G; CARBOHYDRATES: 6G; SUGAR: 1G; FIBER: 1G; SODIUM: 193MG

Chicken and Vegetable Soup with Rice

GLUTEN-FREE | DAIRY-FREE | LOW-FODMAP | SIBO-FRIENDLY | GERD-FRIENDLY

Ground chicken makes this soup really easy to eat. To make the soup low in carbohydrates and sugar, you can omit the rice altogether. You can also add different spices, trying orange, lime, or lemon zest; cumin; or turmeric to add unique flavors to the soup. This freezes well.

SERVES 10
Serving size: ½ cup
Prep time: 10 minutes
Cook time: 25 minutes

———————

1 tablespoon extra-virgin olive oil

3 scallions, green parts only, chopped

10 ounces ground skinless chicken breast

4½ cups Poultry Stock (page 147)

2 carrots, peeled and chopped

4 pieces roasted red pepper (jarred), chopped

1 zucchini, peeled and chopped

½ teaspoon sea salt

1 cup cooked white rice

2 tablespoons chopped fresh tarragon

Ingredient Tip: You can often find cooked white rice in individual servings in the rice aisle or the frozen section of your grocery store.

1. In a large pot, heat the olive oil over medium-high heat until it shimmers.

2. Add the scallions and ground chicken. Cook, crumbling the chicken with your spoon, until the meat is cooked through, about 5 minutes.

3. Add the stock, carrots, red pepper, zucchini, and salt. Simmer the soup, stirring occasionally, until the vegetables are cooked, about 15 minutes.

4. Stir in the rice and tarragon. Serve hot.

 PER SERVING CALORIES: 87; PROTEIN: 8G; TOTAL FAT: 2G; SATURATED FAT: 0G; CARBOHYDRATES: 10G; SUGAR: 1G; FIBER: 1G; SODIUM: 136MG

Cream of Mushroom Soup

GLUTEN-FREE | LOW-CARB | LOW-SUGAR | GERD-FRIENDLY

Soaking the dried mushrooms in warm chicken or vegetable broth gives this soup a deep, earthy, mushroom flavor. While the recipe calls for dried porcini mushrooms (you find them in the produce aisle at most grocery stores), you can use any type of dried mushrooms.

SERVES 10

Serving size: ½ cup
Prep time: 10 minutes,
  plus 1 hour to soak mushrooms
Cook time: 30 minutes

———

4 cups hot Poultry Stock (page 147)
2 ounces dried porcini mushrooms
2 tablespoons extra-virgin olive oil
2 slices turkey bacon, cut into pieces
3 scallions, green parts only, chopped
8 ounces fresh mushrooms, sliced
1 cup peeled and chopped carrots
1 teaspoon dried thyme
½ teaspoon sea salt
¼ cup nonfat milk
2 tablespoons nonfat milk powder

Substitution Tip: To make this soup dairy free, omit the powdered milk and replace the nonfat milk with almond milk.

1. In a medium bowl or glass measuring cup, pour the hot stock over the dried mushrooms. Cover and let the mushrooms to soak for at least 1 hour.

2. Use a slotted spoon to remove the mushrooms from the stock, reserving the stock in the bowl. Finely chop the mushrooms and set aside.

3. In a large pot, heat the olive oil over medium-high heat until it shimmers.

4. Add the bacon and cook for 3 to 5 minutes, stirring occasionally, until it is browned.

5. Add the scallions and fresh mushrooms and cook for 3 to 5 minutes more, stirring occasionally, until the vegetables are soft.

6. Add the stock and reserved mushrooms to the pot, scraping any browned bits from the bottom of the pot with the side of your spoon.

7. Add the carrots, thyme, and salt. Bring to a simmer and cook, stirring occasionally, until the carrots are very soft, about 15 minutes.

8. In a small bowl, whisk together the milk and milk powder.

9. Transfer the milk mixture to the blender along with the hot soup.

10. Blend on high for 1 to 2 minutes until smooth. Serve immediately or return to the pot and reheat before serving if needed.

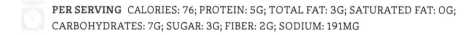 **PER SERVING** CALORIES: 76; PROTEIN: 5G; TOTAL FAT: 3G; SATURATED FAT: 0G; CARBOHYDRATES: 7G; SUGAR: 3G; FIBER: 2G; SODIUM: 191MG

Fennel, Mushroom, and Ground Turkey Soup

GLUTEN-FREE | DAIRY-FREE | LOW-CARB | LOW-SUGAR | GERD-FRIENDLY

Fennel has a lovely, anise-like flavor that enhances the flavors of the mushrooms and ground turkey in this soup. While this is a chunky soup, if you prefer, you can purée all of the other ingredients before adding the cooked turkey meat back in at the end.

SERVES 10
Serving size: ½ cup
Prep time: 10 minutes
Cook time: 25 minutes

———

2 tablespoons extra-virgin olive oil
3 scallions, green parts only, chopped
10 ounces ground skinless turkey breast
4 cups Poultry Stock (page 147)
½ fennel bulb, chopped
8 ounces mushrooms, sliced
2 carrots, peeled and chopped
1 teaspoon dried thyme
½ teaspoon sea salt

Substitution Tip: To add even more nutrients to this soup, stir in a handful of trimmed baby spinach to the pot when you add the turkey at the end.

1. In a large pot, heat the olive oil over medium-high heat until it shimmers.

2. Add the scallions and ground turkey. Cook, crumbling the meat with a spoon, until it is cooked through, about 5 minutes.

3. With a slotted spoon, remove the turkey and onions from the soup and set them aside on a platter.

4. Add the stock, fennel, mushrooms, carrots, thyme, and salt to the pot. Simmer the soup for 10 to 15 minutes, or until the vegetables are very soft.

5. Return the ground turkey to the pot and continue to simmer for 1 minute until the turkey is heated through. Serve immediately.

PER SERVING CALORIES: 78; PROTEIN: 9G; TOTAL FAT: 3G; SATURATED FAT: 0G; CARBOHYDRATES: 4G; SUGAR: 2G; FIBER: 1G; SODIUM: 339MG

New England Clam Chowder

GLUTEN-FREE | DAIRY-FREE

In this version of New England clam chowder, fennel adds a subtle flavor that enhances the sweetness of the clams. The soup calls for sweet rice flour as a thickener. If you aren't sensitive to gluten, you can substitute the rice flour with an equal amount of all-purpose flour.

SERVES 10
Serving size: ½ cup
Prep time: 10 minutes
Cook time: 25 minutes

———

2 tablespoons extra-virgin olive oil
2 slices turkey bacon, cut into pieces
4 scallions, green parts only, chopped
¼ cup chopped fennel
1 carrot, peeled and chopped
2 tablespoons sweet rice flour
4 cups Poultry Stock (page 147)
1 red potato, peeled and chopped
4 pieces roasted red pepper (from a jar),
    chopped (optional)
6 ounces canned clams, drained
½ teaspoon sea salt
½ cup Rice Milk (page 56)
2 tablespoons chopped fennel fronds

Ingredient Tip: When working with fennel, you can use the bulb, stalks, and fronds. To use the bulb, remove the fibrous end and the core and then cut the bulb into small pieces. Chop the stalks as you would celery. The fronds make a lovely addition to soups. Cut the feathery pieces from the stalks and then finely chop them.

1. In a large pot, heat the olive oil over medium-high heat until it shimmers.

2. Add the turkey bacon and cook, stirring occasionally, until it is crisp, about 5 minutes.

3. Remove the turkey bacon from the hot oil with a slotted spoon and set it aside.

4. Add the scallions, fennel, and carrots to the pot and cook, stirring occasionally, until the vegetables begin to brown, about 5 minutes.

5. Add the rice flour and cook, stirring constantly, for 2 minutes.

6. Stir in the stock, scraping up any browned bits from the bottom of the pan with the side of a spoon.

7. Add the potato, red pepper (if using), clams, and salt. Simmer for 10 to 15 minutes until the vegetables are very soft.

8. Stir in the rice milk, reserved turkey bacon, and chopped fennel fronds. Serve immediately.

 PER SERVING CALORIES: 84; PROTEIN: 3G; TOTAL FAT: 3G; SATURATED FAT: 0G; CARBOHYDRATES: 11G; SUGAR: 2G; FIBER: 1G; SODIUM: 262MG

Manhattan Clam Chowder

GLUTEN-FREE | DAIRY-FREE | LOW-CARB | LOW-SUGAR

Unlike its cream-based New England counterpart, Manhattan clam chowder uses a tomato base broth. The result is a light, flavorful soup filled with fragrant herbs and sweet, tender clams. If you can't tolerate clams, replace them with any soft, white-fleshed fish.

SERVES 10
Serving size: ½ cup
Prep time: 10 minutes
Cook time: 20 minutes

———

2 tablespoons extra-virgin olive oil
4 scallions, green parts only, chopped
2 cups Poultry Stock (page 147)
2 cups tomato juice, strained
6 ounces canned clams, with their juice
1 Russet potato, peeled and chopped
2 carrots, peeled and chopped
1 bay leaf
1 teaspoon dried thyme
½ teaspoon sea salt
2 tablespoons chopped flat-leaf parsley

Substitution Tip: Halibut is a very good substitute for clams. To use halibut, remove the skin and cut it into bite sized pieces. Cook it with the scallions in the olive oil in the second step. Remove the halibut with tongs and set it aside, continuing with the recipe. Return the halibut and any juices that have collected back to the pot when you add the parsley, and cook for about 1 minute to warm the fish.

1. In a large pot, heat the olive oil over medium-high heat until it shimmers.

2. Add the scallions and cook, stirring occasionally, until soft, for 1 to 2 minutes.

3. Add the stock, tomato juice, clams with their juice, potato, carrots, bay leaf, thyme, and salt, and simmer over medium heat until the vegetables are very soft, about 15 minutes.

4. Stir in the parsley just before serving.

PER SERVING CALORIES: 63; PROTEIN: 2G; TOTAL FAT: 3G; SATURATED FAT: 0G; CARBOHYDRATES: 8G; SUGAR: 3G; FIBER: 1G; SODIUM: 196MG

Coconut Shrimp Chowder

GLUTEN-FREE | DAIRY-FREE | LOW-FODMAP | LOW-CARB
LOW-SUGAR | SIBO-FRIENDLY | GERD-FRIENDLY

This creamy chowder has a delicious restaurant-quality flavor profile. It freezes well and will keep in the refrigerator for up to three days or the freezer for up to six months. Use light coconut milk that comes in a can, and not the de-flavored coconut milk that comes in a carton, because you want the soup to have a pleasant coconut flavor.

SERVES 10

Serving size: ½ cup
Prep time: 10 minutes
Cook time: 25 minutes

---

2 tablespoons extra-virgin olive oil
4 scallions, green parts only, chopped
2 carrots, peeled and chopped
1 tablespoon grated peeled fresh ginger
2 cups Poultry Stock (page 147)
2 cups light coconut milk
1 sweet potato, peeled and chopped
Juice of 1 lime, strained
Zest of ½ lime
½ teaspoon sea salt
8 ounces cooked baby shrimp
1 tablespoon chopped cilantro

Ingredient Tip: Some people have a genetic predisposition to dislike cilantro because it tastes soapy to them. If you are in that group, feel free to omit the cilantro.

1. In a large pot, heat the olive oil over medium-high heat until it shimmers.

2. Add the scallions, carrots, and ginger. Cook, stirring occasionally, until the carrots soften, about 5 minutes.

3. Add the stock and coconut milk, scraping any browned bits from the bottom of the pan with the side of a spoon.

4. Add the sweet potato, juice, zest, and salt. Bring to a simmer and reduce the heat to medium.

5. Continue to simmer the chowder until the potatoes are soft, 10 to 15 minutes.

6. Stir in the baby shrimp and the cilantro. Cook for 1 to 2 minutes until the shrimp are warmed through. Serve immediately.

 PER SERVING CALORIES: 92; PROTEIN: 6G; TOTAL FAT: 6G; SATURATED FAT: 3G; CARBOHYDRATES: 7G; SUGAR: 2G; FIBER: 1G; SODIUM: 304MG

Fish Stew

GLUTEN-FREE | DAIRY-FREE | LOW-FODMAP | LOW-CARB
LOW-SUGAR | SIBO-FRIENDLY | GERD-FRIENDLY

This simple fish stew is warming and satisfying. While the recipe calls for cod, you can use any white-fleshed fish, such as halibut. The predominant flavors in this dish are orange and tarragon, which work well with the sweet, delicate flavor of the fish.

SERVES 8
Serving size: 1 cup
Prep time: 15 minutes
Cook time: 30 minutes

---

2 tablespoons extra-virgin olive oil
4 scallions, green parts only, chopped
2 carrots, peeled and chopped
1 sweet potato, peeled and chopped
3 cups Poultry Stock (page 147)
Juice of 1 orange, strained
Zest of ½ orange
½ teaspoon sea salt
1 tablespoon dried tarragon
1 pound cod fillets, skin removed
    and cut into 1-inch pieces

Substitution Tip: This stew can also be made in a slow cooker. Add all of the ingredients, except for the fish, to the slow cooker and cook on low for 8 hours. Then, remove the lid and add the fish, and cook on low for 1 more hour with the lid off.

1. In a large pot, heat the olive oil over medium-high heat until it shimmers.

2. Add the scallions and carrots and cook, stirring occasionally, until the vegetables begin to brown, about 5 minutes.

3. Add the sweet potato, stock, juice, zest, salt, and tarragon. Bring the mixture to a simmer and reduce the heat to medium-low.

4. Continue to simmer the stew until the potato is soft, about 15 minutes.

5. Add the cod and simmer for another 5 minutes, stirring occasionally, until the fish is cooked through. Serve immediately.

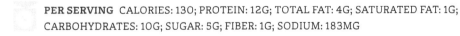

PER SERVING CALORIES: 130; PROTEIN: 12G; TOTAL FAT: 4G; SATURATED FAT: 1G; CARBOHYDRATES: 10G; SUGAR: 5G; FIBER: 1G; SODIUM: 183MG

Chicken-Lime Stew

GLUTEN-FREE | DAIRY-FREE | LOW-CARB | LOW-SUGAR

This Southwest-inspired chicken stew is delicious and satisfying. It's also nutrient dense and loaded with protein. This stew freezes well and reheats easily in the microwave without compromising its flavors at all. If dairy isn't a concern, garnish the stew with a few tablespoons of low-fat cheese and some chopped avocado.

SERVES 8
Serving size: 1 cup
Prep time: 5 minutes
Cook time: 20 minutes

———

2 tablespoons extra-virgin olive oil

4 scallions, green parts only, chopped

1 pound boneless, skinless chicken breast, cut into 1-inch pieces

2 carrots, peeled and chopped

4 ounces mushrooms, halved

1 cup Poultry Stock (page 147)

1 cup strained tomato juice

Juice of 1 lime, strained

Zest of ½ lime

½ teaspoon ground cumin

½ teaspoon ground coriander

½ teaspoon sea salt

2 tablespoons chopped cilantro (optional)

Cooking Tip: You can make this stew in a slow cooker. Combine all of the ingredients in the slow cooker and cook it on low for 8 hours.

1. In a large pot, heat the olive oil over medium-high heat until it shimmers.

2. Add the scallions and chicken and cook, stirring occasionally, for 5 minutes.

3. Add the carrots, mushrooms, stock, tomato juice, lime juice, zest, cumin, coriander, and salt. Bring the stew to a simmer and then reduce the heat to medium.

4. Cook, for 10 to 15 minutes, stirring occasionally, until the carrots and mushrooms are soft.

5. Stir in the chopped cilantro (if using) and serve immediately.

PER SERVING CALORIES: 142; PROTEIN: 19G; TOTAL FAT: 6G; SATURATED FAT: 1G; CARBOHYDRATES: 4G; SUGAR: 2G; FIBER: 1G; SODIUM: 294MG

Chilled Avocado Soup

GLUTEN-FREE | LOW-FODMAP | SIBO-FRIENDLY | GERD-FRIENDLY

This simple soup is refreshing and flavorful, making it perfect for a light summer meal. Because avocados brown so easily, it doesn't keep well, so the soup is best consumed within a few hours of preparation.

SERVES 6

Serving size: 1 cup

Prep time: 10 minutes,
   plus 2 hours to chill

Cook time: None

———

2½ cups Vegetable Stock
   (page 145), chilled

1 avocado, mashed

Juice of 1 orange, strained

Zest of ½ orange

½ teaspoon sea salt

½ teaspoon ground cumin

2 tablespoons chopped cilantro

3 tablespoons nonfat sour cream

Substitution Tip: For a slightly different flavor profile, replace the orange juice and zest with the juice of 2 limes and the zest of ½ a lime.

1. In a blender or food processor, combine the stock, avocado, juice, zest, salt, cumin, and cilantro and process until smooth.

2. Chill for 2 hours before serving.

3. Serve chilled, garnished with sour cream.

PER SERVING CALORIES: 88; PROTEIN: 1G; TOTAL FAT: 7G; SATURATED FAT: 1G; CARBOHYDRATES: 7G; SUGAR: 3G; FIBER: 2G; SODIUM: 402MG

8

VEGETARIAN & VEGAN

Tofu-Rice Stir-Fry

DAIRY-FREE

Marinating silken tofu in a quick soy-based marinade adds flavor to this quick and easy stir-fry. Use pre-cooked white rice, which you can find at your local grocery store in the rice or frozen food aisles. Using pre-cooked rice will save you time and effort.

SERVES 4

Serving size: 1 cup
Prep time: 15 minutes,
   plus 1 hour to marinate
Cook time: 20 minutes

———

2 tablespoons soy sauce
Juice of 1 orange, strained
1 tablespoon grated peeled fresh ginger
¼ teaspoon sesame oil
8 ounces silken tofu, cut into 1-inch pieces
2 tablespoons extra-virgin olive oil
4 scallions, green parts only, chopped
1 carrot, peeled and chopped
1 zucchini, peeled and chopped
4 ounces shiitake mushrooms, chopped
2 cups cooked white rice

Ingredient Tip: To save money, you can pre-cook your own white rice and freeze it in zipper bags in 1-cup servings. This allows you to have cooked rice readily available whenever you need it. A few minutes in the microwave thaws it thoroughly.

1. In a small bowl, whisk together the soy sauce, juice, ginger, and sesame oil. Add the tofu and marinate for 1 hour.

2. Remove the tofu, reserving the marinade, and pat the tofu dry with paper towels.

3. In a large sauté pan, heat the olive oil over medium-high heat. Add the scallions, carrot, zucchini, mushrooms, and tofu. Cook, stirring occasionally, until the vegetables are soft, about 10 minutes.

4. Add the rice and the reserved marinade. Cook for another 4 minutes, and serve hot.

 PER SERVING CALORIES: 340; PROTEIN: 10G; TOTAL FAT: 9G; SATURATED FAT: 1G; CARBOHYDRATES: 55G; SUGAR: 10G; FIBER: 3G; SODIUM: 561MG

Vegetable Fried Rice

DAIRY-FREE | LOW-FODMAP | SIBO-FRIENDLY | GERD-FRIENDLY

Scrambled eggs add protein to this fried rice, although you can omit it or replace the egg with tofu if you are vegan. Butternut squash adds vitamins A and C, while soy sauce adds flavor. To make the dish gluten-free, select a gluten-free soy sauce, such as tamari.

SERVES 4

Serving size: 1 cup
Prep time: 15 minutes
Cook time: 20 minutes

----

2 tablespoons olive oil
4 scallions, green parts only, chopped
1 tablespoon grated peeled fresh ginger
1 cup cubed butternut squash
4 eggs, lightly beaten
2 cups baby spinach, trimmed
2 tablespoons soy sauce
Juice of 1 lime, strained
2 cups cooked white rice
2 tablespoons chopped cilantro

Substitution Tip: To make this dish lower in carbohydrates, replace the white rice with zucchini "rice." To make zucchini rice, place chunks of peeled zucchini in a food processor. Pulse the chunks for 5 or 6 one-second bursts until the zucchini resembles rice.

1. In a large sauté pan, heat the olive oil over medium-high heat until it shimmers.

2. Add the scallions, ginger, and squash and cook, stirring occasionally, until the squash is soft, about 10 minutes.

3. Add the eggs and cook for 1 to 2 minutes, stirring constantly, until the eggs are set.

4. Add the spinach, soy sauce, and juice, and cook, stirring occasionally, until the spinach wilts, about 2 more minutes.

5. Add the white rice, and cook stirring occasionally, until the rice is heated through, about 3 minutes more.

6. Stir in the cilantro. Serve immediately.

PER SERVING CALORIES: 319; PROTEIN: 10G; TOTAL FAT: 12G; SATURATED FAT: 3G; CARBOHYDRATES: 43G; SUGAR: 2G; FIBER: 2G; SODIUM: 530MG

Quinoa with Veggies

GLUTEN-FREE | DAIRY-FREE

Colorful beets and carrots lend a pretty color to this quinoa, and add an earthy sweetness. Using canned beets ensures the vegetables are soft and well cooked, and therefore more easily tolerated. To add protein, toss in a few ounces of silken tofu or a scrambled egg.

SERVES 6

Serving size: ½ cup
Prep time: 15 minutes
Cook time: 25 minutes

---

2 tablespoons extra-virgin olive oil
4 scallions, green parts only, chopped
1 carrot, peeled and chopped
¼ cup drained and chopped
    canned beets
½ teaspoon sea salt
2 cups Vegetable Stock (page 145)
1 cup uncooked quinoa
1 tablespoon chopped fresh parsley
    (optional)

Ingredient Tip: There are multiple types of quinoa, and it comes in many colors. Any type of uncooked quinoa works well in this recipe. Be sure to wash your quinoa extremely well, as unwashed quinoa is coated with natural saponins, a soapy substance that some people cannot tolerate.

1. In a medium pot, heat the olive oil over medium-high heat until it shimmers.

2. Add the scallions and carrot and cook, stirring occasionally, until the vegetables begin to brown, about 5 minutes.

3. Add the beets, salt, stock, and quinoa, and bring the mixture to a boil.

4. Reduce the heat to low, cover the pot, and simmer for 20 minutes, until the quinoa is soft.

5. Fluff the quinoa with a fork and stir in the parsley (if using). Serve hot.

 PER SERVING CALORIES: 160; PROTEIN: 4G; TOTAL FAT: 6G; SATURATED FAT: 1G; CARBOHYDRATES: 22G; SUGAR: 2G; FIBER: 3G; SODIUM: 400MG

Cinnamon Rice and Veggie Bowl

GLUTEN-FREE | DAIRY-FREE

Cinnamon and other sweet spices add unique flavor to this delicious rice and vegetable bowl. Use pre-cooked rice to make the recipe quick and easy. Feel free to choose any vegetables that will work well for your condition, substituting as needed.

SERVES 4
Serving size: 1 cup
Prep time: 10 minutes
Cook time: 10 minutes

---

2 tablespoons extra-virgin olive oil
4 scallions, green parts only, chopped
1 carrot, peeled and chopped
1 cup peeled, seeded, and finely
    chopped butternut squash
¼ cup Vegetable Stock (page 145)
1½ cups cooked white rice
½ teaspoon sea salt
½ teaspoon ground cinnamon
¼ teaspoon ground nutmeg
¼ teaspoon ground ginger

Substitution Tip: You can also make this as a breakfast dish, substituting the onions and vegetables with fruits that work well for you, such as peeled peaches, apples, or plums.

1. In a large sauté pan, heat the olive oil on medium-high until it shimmers.

2. Add the scallions, carrot, and squash and cook, stirring occasionally, until the vegetables begin to brown, about 5 minutes.

3. Add the stock, rice, salt, cinnamon, nutmeg, and ginger.

4. Cook, stirring occasionally, for 5 minutes. Serve immediately.

PER SERVING CALORIES: 216; PROTEIN: 3G; TOTAL FAT: 7G; SATURATED FAT: 1G; CARBOHYDRATES: 35G; SUGAR: 2G; FIBER: 2G; SODIUM: 342MG

Butternut Squash Orzo

DAIRY-FREE

Orzo is a rice-shaped pasta. In this recipe, the orzo is cooked risotto style. Cooking the orzo in stock helps release the starches and makes it creamy. If you can tolerate dairy, you can stir in a little bit of grated Parmesan cheese at the end to give it a creamier flavor.

SERVES 6
Serving size: 1 cup
Prep time: 10 minutes
Cook time: 20 minutes

———

1 tablespoon extra-virgin olive oil
2 scallions, green parts only, chopped
1½ cups peeled, seeded, and finely chopped butternut squash
¾ cup orzo
3 cups Vegetable Stock (page 145)
½ teaspoon sea salt
1 teaspoon dried sage
1 tablespoon chopped fresh parsley (optional)

Ingredient Tip: You can use any type of winter squash in this dish, or try it with carrots or zucchini in place of the squash.

1. In a large sauté pan, heat the olive oil on medium-high until it shimmers.

2. Add the scallions and squash and cook, stirring occasionally, until the vegetables start to brown, about 5 minutes.

3. Add the orzo and cook, stirring constantly, for 1 minute.

4. Add the vegetable stock, salt, and sage. Cook, stirring occasionally, until the orzo is soft, about 10 minutes.

5. Stir in the parsley (if using). Serve hot.

 PER SERVING CALORIES: 125; PROTEIN: 3G; TOTAL FAT: 3G; SATURATED FAT: 0G; CARBOHYDRATES: 22G; SUGAR: 4G; FIBER: 2G; SODIUM: 288MG

Savory Asparagus and Mushroom Porridge

DAIRY-FREE

This recipe turns a breakfast staple into a savory meal. If you eat dairy, you can add a little bit of umami flavor by stirring in a few tablespoons of Parmesan cheese at the end of cooking. Using vegetable stock also adds rich flavors to the porridge. To make this porridge gluten-free, replace the Cream of Wheat with rice that you've processed in a food processor into a meal.

SERVES 4
Serving size: 1 cup
Prep time: 15 minutes
Cook time: 15 minutes

———————

2 tablespoons extra-virgin olive oil
4 scallions, green parts only, chopped
8 ounces mushrooms, sliced
8 asparagus spears, peeled and chopped
1 teaspoon dried thyme
½ teaspoon sea salt
2 cups Vegetable Stock (page 145)
⅓ cup Cream of Wheat cereal

Ingredient Tip: To prepare the asparagus, hold each end of a stalk of asparagus between two fingers and bend it until it snaps. Discard the fibrous end. Use a vegetable peeler to remove the outer peel of the stalks, leaving only the tender vegetable inside.

1. In a medium pot, heat the olive oil over medium-high heat until it shimmers.

2. Add the scallions, mushrooms, asparagus, thyme, and salt and cook for 5 to 7 minutes, stirring occasionally, until the mushrooms are browned.

3. Add the stock and bring the liquid to a boil.

4. Stirring constantly, pour the Cream of Wheat into the pot in a steady but thin stream. Cook for 2 to 3 minutes, continuing to stir constantly, until the porridge thickens. Serve hot.

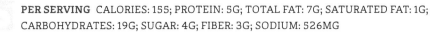 **PER SERVING** CALORIES: 155; PROTEIN: 5G; TOTAL FAT: 7G; SATURATED FAT: 1G; CARBOHYDRATES: 19G; SUGAR: 4G; FIBER: 3G; SODIUM: 526MG

Tofu and Root Vegetable Pie

DAIRY-FREE

This recipe uses Root Vegetable Purée (page 81) for the top of a pie filled with savory mushroom, tofu, and vegetable. It's a satisfying and filling meal for a cool evening. If you consume dairy, consider stirring a little bit of Parmesan cheese into the purée to add a savory flavor.

SERVES 8
Serving size: ⅛ pie
Prep time: 15 minutes
Cook time: 20 minutes

———————

2 tablespoons extra-virgin olive oil
4 scallions, green parts only, chopped
12 ounces silken tofu, cut into pieces
4 ounces mushrooms, sliced
2 carrots, chopped
2 cups baby spinach, trimmed
Dash ground nutmeg
2 tablespoons flour
2 cups Vegetable Stock (page 145)
2 tablespoons soy sauce
½ teaspoon dried thyme
½ teaspoon sea salt
Root Vegetable Purée (page 81)

Ingredient Tip: Silken tofu contains quite a bit of water. If you prefer your tofu a little firmer, put it in a colander with a plate set on top and allow the water to drain off for about 30 minutes before cutting it into pieces.

1. Preheat the broiler.

2. In a large sauté pan, heat the olive oil on medium-high until it shimmers.

3. Add the scallions, tofu, mushrooms, and carrots and cook, stirring occasionally, until the vegetables are soft, about 5 minutes.

4. Add the baby spinach and nutmeg. Cook, stirring constantly, for 1 minute more.

5. Add the flour and cook, stirring constantly, for 1 minute.

6. Add the stock, soy sauce, thyme, and salt and bring to a simmer. Cook, stirring frequently, for about 5 minutes more.

7. Transfer the mixture to a 9-inch pie pan. Spread the purée over the top of the vegetables.

8. Broil for 2 to 3 minutes until the purée browns.

 PER SERVING CALORIES: 305; PROTEIN: 13G; TOTAL FAT: 16G; SATURATED FAT: 5G; CARBOHYDRATES: 30G; SUGAR: 13G; FIBER: 7G; SODIUM: 1485MG

Sweet Potato–Coconut Stew

GLUTEN-FREE | DAIRY-FREE | LOW-FODMAP | SIBO-FRIENDLY

Curry lovers will enjoy this vegan stew, but choose a mild curry powder. If you can't tolerate curry, it's okay to leave it out; substitute cinnamon and nutmeg to give the stew a little more flavor. Tasty sweet potatoes add nutrients and make the stew satisfying and delicious.

SERVES 4

Serving size: 1 cup
Prep time: 10 minutes
Cook time: 30 minutes

---

2 tablespoons extra-virgin olive oil

4 scallions, green parts only, chopped

2 cups baby spinach, trimmed

2 sweet potatoes, peeled and cubed

2 cups Vegetable Stock (page 145)

1 cup light coconut milk

½ teaspoon curry powder

½ teaspoon ground cumin

½ teaspoon sea salt

Zest of ½ lime

1 tablespoon chopped cilantro

Substitution Tip: Lime and coconut are a classic flavor combination, but if you'd like to change things up a bit, try using orange zest in place of the lime zest, which complements the flavors in the sweet potatoes.

1. In a large pot, heat the olive oil over medium-high heat until it shimmers.

2. Add the scallions and spinach and cook, stirring frequently, until the spinach is wilted, about 2 minutes.

3. Add the sweet potatoes, stock, coconut milk, curry powder, cumin, salt, and zest. Bring the mixture to a simmer and then reduce the temperature to medium-low.

4. Continue to simmer the stew for 15 to 20 minutes until the sweet potatoes are soft.

5. Stir in the cilantro. Serve immediately.

PER SERVING CALORIES: 200; PROTEIN: 3G; TOTAL FAT: 10G; SATURATED FAT: 4G; CARBOHYDRATES: 27G; SUGAR: 2G; FIBER: 4G; SODIUM: 747MG

Veggie Pasta

DAIRY-FREE | LOW-FODMAP | LOW-CARB | LOW-SUGAR | SIBO-FRIENDLY

This simple garden pasta combines fresh-flavored vegetables and herbs to make a tasty tomato-based sauce. While the recipe calls for spaghetti, you can use any pasta you'd like. Use any summer squash that is available, such as pattypan squash or zucchini.

SERVES 8

Serving size: 1 ounce pasta
   and ½ cup sauce
Prep time: 15 minutes
Cook time: 20 minutes

---

2 tablespoons extra-virgin olive oil

4 scallions, green parts only, chopped

1 yellow crookneck or pattypan squash,
   peeled and cubed

2 carrots, peeled and chopped

1 zucchini, peeled and cubed

4 ounces mushrooms, sliced

2 cups tomato juice, strained

1 teaspoon dried oregano

½ teaspoon dried marjoram

½ teaspoon dried thyme

½ teaspoon sea salt

2 tablespoons chopped fresh basil

8 ounces pasta, cooked according to
   package directions

Substitution Tip: If you'd like to lower the carbohydrate count and make this gluten-free, then substitute zucchini noodles for the spaghetti. Use a vegetable peeler to cut the zucchini into strips and a knife to cut it into noodles. Sauté in a little olive oil for about 5 minutes to soften it.

1. In a large pot, heat the olive oil over medium-high heat until it shimmers.

2. Add the scallions, squash, carrots, zucchini, and mushrooms and cook until the vegetables begin to soften, about 5 minutes.

3. Add the tomato juice, oregano, marjoram, thyme, and salt. Bring the sauce to a simmer and reduce the heat to medium-low. Continue to simmer for 10 to 15 minutes, stirring occasionally, until the vegetables are very soft.

4. Serve the pasta topped with the sauce.

 PER SERVING CALORIES: 141; PROTEIN: 5G; TOTAL FAT: 4G; SATURATED FAT: 1G; CARBOHYDRATES: 22G; SUGAR: 4G; FIBER: 2G; SODIUM: 333MG

Asparagus Quiche

GLUTEN-FREE | LOW-CARB | LOW-SUGAR

Peeling and cooking the asparagus ahead of time will make it very soft in this quiche, making it easier to digest. Leaving the quiche crustless makes it low in carbohydrates, so it's diabetic-friendly. If you'd like to make the recipe dairy free, eliminate the Parmesan cheese and substitute a nondairy milk (such as the Almond Milk on page 57).

SERVES 8
Serving size: ⅛ pie
Prep time: 15 minutes
Cook time: 35 minutes

Nonstick cooking spray
8 spears asparagus, peeled and cut
    into pieces
6 eggs
½ cup nonfat milk
¼ cup grated Parmesan cheese
2 tablespoons chopped fresh basil
½ teaspoon lemon zest
½ teaspoon sea salt
2 tablespoons finely chopped roasted
    red peppers (from a jar)

*Substitution Tip: Try substituting
thinly sliced zucchini or summer
squash for the asparagus.*

1. Preheat the oven to 350°F. Spray a 9-inch pie plate with nonstick cooking spray.

2. Fill a large pot with water and bring it to a boil.

3. Add the chopped asparagus and boil for 3 minutes. Drain the asparagus in a colander and then run it under cold water to stop the cooking and cool the vegetables.

4. In a large bowl, whisk together the eggs, milk, cheese, basil, zest, and salt.

5. Fold in the asparagus and roasted red peppers.

6. Pour the mixture into the prepared pie pan. Bake for 25 to 30 minutes until set.

PER SERVING CALORIES: 75; PROTEIN: 7G; TOTAL FAT: 5G; SATURATED FAT: 2G; CARBOHYDRATES: 2G; SUGAR: 0G; FIBER: 2G; SODIUM: 218MG

Spinach Quiche

GLUTEN-FREE | LOW-CARB | LOW-SUGAR | SIBO-FRIENDLY | GERD-FRIENDLY

Tender baby spinach adds flavor and nutrients to this protein-rich quiche. Leaving off the crust eliminates gluten and makes this low-carbohydrate meal helpful for people with diabetes seeking to control blood sugar. Sautéing the spinach lightly before adding it softens the greens.

SERVES 8

Serving size: ⅛ pie
Prep time: 15 minutes
Cook time: 35 minutes

Nonstick cooking spray
2 tablespoons extra-virgin olive oil
4 scallions, green parts only, chopped
3 cups baby spinach, trimmed
½ teaspoon orange zest
¼ teaspoon ground nutmeg
1 teaspoon dried tarragon
½ teaspoon sea salt
6 eggs
½ cup nonfat milk
½ cup grated low-fat Swiss cheese

Ingredient Tip: Freshly grated nutmeg has much better flavor than the pre-grated spice. You can find whole nutmeg in many spice aisles. To grate it, use a rasp-style grater.

1. Preheat the oven to 350°F. Spray a 9-inch pie plate with nonstick cooking spray.

2. In a large sauté pan, heat the olive oil over medium-high heat until it shimmers.

3. Add the scallions and spinach and cook for 2 to 3 minutes, stirring occasionally, until the spinach wilts. Remove the vegetables from the heat and let cool.

4. In a large bowl, whisk together the zest, nutmeg, tarragon, salt, eggs, and milk until mixed well.

5. Fold in the cheese and spinach-scallion mixture.

6. Pour the mixture into the prepared pie plate. Bake for 25 to 30 minutes in the preheated oven until the quiche sets.

 PER SERVING CALORIES: 111; PROTEIN: 7G; TOTAL FAT: 8G; SATURATED FAT: 3G; CARBOHYDRATES: 2G; SUGAR: 1G; FIBER: 0G; SODIUM: 209MG

Easy Slow Cooker Strata

GERD-FRIENDLY

This recipe takes almost no time at all to prepare. It makes a wonderful breakfast or dinner, and it reheats well in the microwave. You can also freeze it in single portions to take for meals on the go, so it's a perfect meal to make on the weekend and eat throughout the week.

SERVES 8

Serving size: ½ cup
Prep time: 15 minutes
Cook time: 8 hours

———————

4 whole eggs
8 egg whites
1½ cups nonfat milk
½ teaspoon sea salt
½ teaspoon dried thyme
2 tablespoons chopped roasted red
   peppers (from a jar)
1 zucchini, peeled and chopped
1 cup sliced mushrooms
½ cup nonfat Cheddar cheese
8 slices white bread, crust removed
   and cut into cubes

Substitution Tip: Fold in 1 cup of frozen or fresh baby spinach along with the other vegetables for extra flavor and nutrition.

1. In a large bowl, whisk together the eggs, egg whites, milk, salt, and thyme.

2. Fold in the roasted red peppers, zucchini, mushrooms, and cheese.

3. Place the bread cubes in a slow cooker. Pour the egg mixture over the bread, covering it completely and stir to combine.

4. Turn the slow cooker on low and cook for 6 to 8 hours, until the eggs are set.

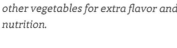 **PER SERVING** CALORIES: 125; PROTEIN: 11G; TOTAL FAT: 5G; SATURATED FAT: 2G; CARBOHYDRATES: 9G; SUGAR: 4G; FIBER: 1G; SODIUM: 321MG

Baked Mushroom Risotto

GLUTEN-FREE | LOW-FODMAP | LOW-CARB | LOW-SUGAR
SIBO-FRIENDLY | GERD-FRIENDLY

Risotto is a creamy rice dish made with Arborio rice, an extra-starchy rice from Italy. This savory version mixes mushrooms and herbs, and it's easy to make because you don't have to spend 30 minutes at the stove stirring. Instead, you bake this risotto, making it an easy weeknight meal.

SERVES 8

Serving size: ½ cup
Prep time: 15 minutes,
   plus 1 hour to soak mushrooms
Cook time: 35 minutes

2¾ cups hot Vegetable Stock (page 145)
2 ounces dried porcini mushrooms
2 tablespoons extra-virgin olive oil
4 scallions, green parts only, chopped
8 ounces mushrooms, sliced
¾ cup Arborio rice
1 teaspoon dried thyme
½ teaspoon sea salt
¼ cup nonfat cream cheese

Ingredient Tip: You will sometimes find Arborio rice labeled as risotto rice in the grocery store.

1. In a medium bowl or a glass measuring cup, pour the hot stock over the porcini mushrooms. Allow them to soak for at least 1 hour.

2. Remove the mushrooms from the bowl, reserving the stock. Finely chop the mushrooms.

3. Preheat the oven to 425°F.

4. In a large ovenproof pot, heat the olive oil over medium-high heat until it shimmers.

5. Add the scallions and dried and fresh mushrooms and cook for 5 to 7 minutes, stirring occasionally, until the mushrooms are browned.

6. Add the rice and cook, stirring constantly, for 2 minutes.

7. Stir in the reserved stock, thyme, and salt. Bring the rice mixture to a boil, stirring occasionally.

8. Cover the pot and transfer it to the preheated oven. Cook for 20 to 25 minutes until the liquid is completely absorbed.

9. Remove the risotto from the oven. Uncover and stir in the cream cheese. Serve immediately.

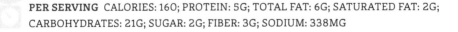

PER SERVING CALORIES: 160; PROTEIN: 5G; TOTAL FAT: 6G; SATURATED FAT: 2G; CARBOHYDRATES: 21G; SUGAR: 2G; FIBER: 3G; SODIUM: 338MG

Baked Eggs Florentine

GLUTEN-FREE | DAIRY-FREE | LOW-FODMAP | LOW-CARB | LOW-SUGAR | SIBO-FRIENDLY

Baking the eggs in individual custard cups makes this easy dish to take with you and reheat. This simple recipe is low in carbohydrates, so it's great for people with diabetes looking for a vegetarian meal and also seeking to control their blood sugar. The eggs are high in protein, and the spinach adds plenty of vitamins.

SERVES 4
Serving size: 1 custard cup
Prep time: 15 minutes
Cook time: 20 minutes

Nonstick cooking spray
2 tablespoons extra-virgin olive oil
4 scallions, green parts only, chopped
6 cups baby spinach, trimmed
¼ teaspoon ground nutmeg
¼ teaspoon orange zest
Juice of ½ orange, strained
½ teaspoon sea salt
4 eggs

Cooking Tip: It may be easier to crack the eggs into a custard cup and then pour it from the cup into the ramekin. Otherwise, egg may roll down the side of the ramekin.

1. Preheat the oven to 375°F. Spray 4 ramekins with nonstick cooking spray.

2. In a large sauté pan, heat the olive oil on medium-high until it shimmers.

3. Add the scallions and spinach. Cook, stirring occasionally, for 2 minutes.

4. Add the nutmeg, zest, juice, and salt. Cook for another 1 to 2 minutes, until the juice evaporates.

5. Spoon the spinach mixture into the prepared ramekins.

6. Carefully crack an egg on top of the spinach.

7. Bake for 10 to 15 minutes in the preheated oven until the eggs set.

PER SERVING CALORIES: 169; PROTEIN: 8G; TOTAL FAT: 12G; SATURATED FAT: 2G; CARBOHYDRATES: 10G; SUGAR: 7G; FIBER: 1G; SODIUM: 335MG

9

POULTRY
& FISH

Orange-Tarragon Scallops

GLUTEN-FREE | LOW-CARB | LOW-SUGAR

Scallops have a sweet, mild flavor and a soft texture. When properly cooked, the scallops are tender and delicious. However, scallops do have a rubbery membrane that runs along the side of the meat. Use a sharp paring knife to remove this membrane before cooking the scallops.

SERVES 4
Serving size: 2 scallops
Prep time: 10 minutes
Cook time: 15 minutes

---

8 large sea scallops
Sea salt
1 tablespoon extra-virgin olive oil
Juice of 1 orange, strained
Zest of ½ an orange
1 tablespoon dried tarragon
1 tablespoon of cold unsalted butter, cut into pieces

Ingredient Tip: Select scallops that have a milky color. The scallops shouldn't have any fishy odor at all. If they do, then they are past their prime.

1. Pat the scallops dry and season them with salt.

2. In a large sauté pan over medium-high heat, heat the olive oil until it shimmers.

3. Add the scallops and cook, without moving them, until they are each browned on one side, about 3 minutes.

4. Use tongs to flip the scallops. Cook until browned on the second side, about 3 minutes.

5. Remove the scallops from the pan with tongs and set them on a platter. Add the juice, zest, and tarragon to the pan. Bring to a simmer and cook for 1 to 2 minutes, until the liquid reduces by half.

6. Swirl in the butter, stirring constantly until it melts.

7. Return the scallops to the pan, turning them to coat with the pan sauce. Serve immediately.

 PER SERVING CALORIES: 117; PROTEIN: 10G; TOTAL FAT: 7G; SATURATED FAT: 2G; CARBOHYDRATES: 3G; SUGAR: 1G; FIBER: 0G; SODIUM: 176MG

Crab Quiche

GLUTEN-FREE | LOW-FODMAP | LOW-CARB | LOW-SUGAR
SIBO-FRIENDLY | GERD-FRIENDLY

This simple, crustless crab quiche is low in carbohydrates and sugar, and high in protein. It stores and reheats well, so it makes a good lunch on the go, and you can freeze it in individual servings for up to six months. To make it dairy-free, use Almond Milk (page 57) and omit the cheese.

SERVES 8
Serving size: ⅛ pie
Prep time: 15 minutes
Cook time: 25 minutes

———————

Nonstick cooking spray
6 eggs, beaten
½ cup nonfat milk
2 teaspoons dried tarragon
½ teaspoon sea salt
8 ounces cooked lump crab meat,
    rinsed and picked over
¼ cup low-fat Cheddar cheese

Ingredient Tip: Whenever you use lump crab meat, pick it over for any bits of shell that might be in with the meat. Put the crab in a colander and run your fingers through it, feeling for and removing any hard or sharp pieces.

1. Preheat the oven to 350°F. Spray a 9-inch pie plate with nonstick cooking spray.

2. In medium bowl, beat the eggs, milk, tarragon, and salt until well combined.

3. Fold in the crab and cheese.

4. Pour into the prepared pie plate. Bake for 20 to 25 minutes until set.

PER SERVING CALORIES: 88; PROTEIN: 10G; TOTAL FAT: 7G; SATURATED FAT: 2G; CARBOHYDRATES: 2G; SUGAR: 1G; FIBER: 0G; SODIUM: 353MG

Shrimp and "Grits"

GLUTEN-FREE | GERD-FRIENDLY

This Southern classic, generally made with hominy (corn), doesn't need to be beyond the reach of people with gastroparesis. This recipe makes the cheesy grits with rice instead, so it's lower in fiber and easier on your stomach.

SERVES 8
Serving size: ½ cup grits, ¼ cup shrimp
Prep time: 15 minutes
Cook time: 20 minutes

———————

1 cup uncooked white rice
4 cups Fish Stock (page 146)
½ cup nonfat milk
½ teaspoon sea salt
¼ cup low-fat Parmesan cheese
2 tablespoons extra-virgin olive oil
1 pound small shrimp,
    peeled and deveined
2 tablespoons chopped Italian parsley

Ingredient Tip: To devein shrimp, use a sharp paring knife and run it under the vein that runs along the back of the shrimp, pulling the vein away from the shrimp.

1. In a blender or food processor, process the rice for 10 to 15 short pulses, until it is well ground.

2. In a large pot, bring the fish stock, milk, and salt to a slow boil over medium-high heat.

3. Add the rice to the liquid in a thin stream, stirring constantly.

4. Once the rice is all added, cover the pot and simmer the mixture for 4 minutes, or until it is thick and cooked.

5. While the rice cooks, in a large saute pan, heat the olive oil on medium-high until it shimmers.

6. Add the shrimp to the pan and cook, stirring occasionally, until the shrimp is pink, about 4 minutes.

7. When the rice mixture is finished cooking, add the Parmesan cheese to the "grits" and remove the pot from the heat.

8. Once the shrimp is cooked, add the parsley to the pan and stir.

9. Serve the "grits" topped with the shrimp.

 PER SERVING CALORIES: 196; PROTEIN: 16G; TOTAL FAT: 6G; SATURATED FAT: 1G; CARBOHYDRATES: 20G; SUGAR: 2G; FIBER: 0G; SODIUM: 739MG

Steamer Clams with Rice

GLUTEN-FREE | DAIRY-FREE | LOW-FODMAP | SIBO-FRIENDLY | GERD-FRIENDLY

The broth from the clams flavors the rice, making it a uniquely delicious meal. To serve, spoon the clams and fragrant broth over the rice. Save time by using pre-cooked rice. Be sure to put out a bowl so people can discard their shells.

SERVES 4

Serving size: ¼ cup rice, ¼ cup sauce,
   4 ounces clams (in shells)
Prep time: 10 minutes
Cook time: 15 minutes

———

2 tablespoons extra-virgin olive oil
4 scallions, green parts only, chopped
2 carrots, peeled and minced
1 cup Fish Stock (page 146)
½ teaspoon lemon zest
½ teaspoon sea salt
1 teaspoon dried tarragon
1 pound steamer clams,
   rinsed and drained
1 cup cooked white rice

Ingredient Tip: Choose fresh clams with closed shells. After cooking, discard any clams that do not open.

1. In a large pot, heat the olive oil on medium-high until it shimmers.

2. Add the scallions and carrots and cook, stirring occasionally, until the carrots are soft, about 5 minutes.

3. Add the stock, zest, salt, and tarragon. Bring to a simmer.

4. Add the clams. Cover and steam until the clams open, 5 to 10 minutes.

 PER SERVING CALORIES: 227; PROTEIN: 4G; TOTAL FAT: 8G; SATURATED FAT: 1G; CARBOHYDRATES: 35G; SUGAR: 6G; FIBER: 2G; SODIUM: 760MG

Poached Cod
with Blackberry Sauce

GLUTEN-FREE | LOW-CARB | LOW-SUGAR

Blackberry sauce scented with thyme gives this poached cod one-of-a-kind flavor. While this recipe calls for poaching the cod in broth, you can also poach it in water to save money. Serve with the Root Vegetable Purée on page 81.

SERVES 4

Serving size: 2 ounces of cod
Prep time: 15 minutes
Cook time: 20 minutes

---

5 cups Fish Stock (page 146), divided
Zest of 1 lemon
1 teaspoon sea salt, divided
8 ounces cod, cut into 2-ounce pieces,
    skin removed
1 tablespoon extra-virgin olive oil
4 scallions, green parts only, chopped
2 cups blackberries
1 teaspoon dried thyme
1 tablespoon cold unsalted butter,
    cut into pieces

Substitution Tip: You can also make this sauce with blueberries or raspberries for a different flavor. The cod can be replaced with any white-fleshed fish.

1. In a large pot, bring 4 cups fish stock, the zest, and ½ teaspoon salt to a simmer over medium-high heat.

2. Add the cod, ensuring it is completely covered by the liquid, and reduce the temperature to medium-low. Poach the fish until it is fork tender, about 7 minutes.

3. While the cod poaches, in a medium pot, heat the olive oil on medium-high until it shimmers.

4. Add the scallions and cook, stirring occasionally, for 3 minutes.

5. Add the blackberries, the remaining 1 cup of fish stock, the remaining ½ teaspoon of salt, and the thyme. Bring the mixture to a boil. Reduce the heat to medium and simmer for 5 minutes, stirring occasionally.

6. Swirl in the butter until just melted.

7. Strain the sauce through a fine-mesh sieve, removing all of the solids. Spoon on top of the cod, and serve.

 PER SERVING CALORIES: 201; PROTEIN: 21G; TOTAL FAT: 10G; SATURATED FAT: 3G; CARBOHYDRATES: 8G; SUGAR: 4G; FIBER: 4G; SODIUM: 990MG

Cod Poached in Tomato Sauce

GLUTEN-FREE | DAIRY-FREE | LOW-CARB | LOW-SUGAR

Poaching the cod in a flavorful tomato sauce yields a tender, flaky, and tasty fish. You can serve the cod with a little of the poaching liquid spooned over the top. This will work with any white-fleshed fish, such as halibut or tilapia. Serve with the Creamed Spinach on page 86.

SERVES 4

Serving size: 2 ounces of cod

Prep time: 15 minutes

Cook time: 15 minutes

---

2 tablespoons extra-virgin olive oil

4 scallions, green parts only, chopped

4 cups tomato juice, strained

1 teaspoon dried oregano

1 tablespoon chopped fresh basil

½ teaspoon sea salt

8 ounces cod, skin removed and cut into 2-ounce pieces

Substitution Tip: If you tolerate spice well, try adding a dash of Tabasco or other hot sauce to the tomato sauce to give the fish a little zip.

1. In a medium pot, heat the olive oil on medium-high until it shimmers.

2. Add the scallions and cook, stirring occasionally, until soft, about 3 minutes.

3. Ad the tomato juice, oregano, basil, and salt. Bring the liquid to a simmer and reduce the heat to medium.

4. Add the cod and cook until the fish is flaky, about 7 minutes. Serve immediately.

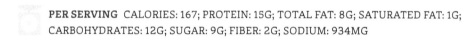

PER SERVING CALORIES: 167; PROTEIN: 15G; TOTAL FAT: 8G; SATURATED FAT: 1G; CARBOHYDRATES: 12G; SUGAR: 9G; FIBER: 2G; SODIUM: 934MG

Halibut with Lemon and Dill

GLUTEN-FREE | DAIRY-FREE | LOW-CARB | LOW-SUGAR | GERD-FRIENDLY

Baking halibut in simple foil packets makes the fish extremely moist, as it steams while it's in the oven. While it's steaming, the flavors of lemon and dill infuse the delicately flavored halibut.

SERVES 4

Serving size: 2 ounces halibut
Prep time: 15 minutes
Cook time: 15 minutes

———————

8 ounces halibut, skin removed
    and cut into 2-ounce pieces
Sea salt
8 dill sprigs
4 lemon slices
1 cup Fish Stock (page 146)

Substitution Tip: If you'd like to make an entire meal in the foil packet, add some peeled and sliced zucchini to the packet. It will steam with the fish.

1. Preheat the oven to 400°F. Put 4 large pieces of aluminum foil on a baking sheet.

2. Season the halibut with salt.

3. Put each halibut piece on a piece of foil. Top the halibut with 2 dill sprigs and 1 lemon slice each.

4. Fold the foil into a packet around the fish, leaving room at the top for a seal.

5. Carefully pour ¼ cup fish stock into each packet, and then seal the packet shut. Place the packets on the baking sheet.

6. Bake in the preheated oven until the halibut is tender, 10 to 15 minutes.

7. Using caution (as steam will be hot), open each packet. Discard the lemon slices and dill springs, and transfer each fish piece to a plate to serve.

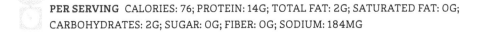 **PER SERVING** CALORIES: 76; PROTEIN: 14G; TOTAL FAT: 2G; SATURATED FAT: 0G; CARBOHYDRATES: 2G; SUGAR: 0G; FIBER: 0G; SODIUM: 184MG

Salmon and Summer Squash in Parchment

Salmon cooked in parchment yields moist, tender fish. You can find parchment paper in the foil aisle at your grocery store. The recipe calls for pre-steaming the squash so it is very tender, but you can also try cooking it directly in the parchment without steaming first, if you can tolerate your vegetables a little more firm.

SERVES 4

Serving size: 2 ounces halibut
Prep time: 15 minutes
Cook time: 30 minutes

———————

1 medium zucchini, peeled and sliced
1 medium yellow summer squash,
    peeled and sliced
8 ounces salmon, skin removed and
    cut into 2-ounce pieces
4 lemon wedges
½ teaspoon sea salt
½ teaspoon dill
½ teaspoon dried thyme

Substitution Tip: This recipe works well with any type of fish, such as trout or halibut.

1. Preheat the oven to 400°F. Put 4 large pieces of parchment paper on a large baking sheet.

2. In a medium pot fitted with a steamer basket, steam the zucchini and summer squash over boiling water for 5 minutes.

3. Put each salmon piece on one piece of parchment. Squeeze 1 lemon wedge over each salmon piece. Sprinkle them with salt, dill, and thyme, and then top them with the cooked zucchini and summer squash.

4. Fold and seal the parchment around the salmon and squash, making 4 packets.

5. Bake in the preheated oven for 20 to 25 minutes until the salmon is opaque.

PER SERVING CALORIES: 93; PROTEIN: 12G; TOTAL FAT: 4G; SATURATED FAT: 1G; CARBOHYDRATES: 4G; SUGAR: 2G; FIBER: 1G; SODIUM: 265MG

Maple-Soy Baked Salmon

GLUTEN-FREE | DAIRY-FREE | GERD-FRIENDLY

Salmon is an earthy, sweet-fleshed fish that pairs very well with maple. Be sure to use pure maple syrup in this recipe, not pancake syrup; the latter is a sugar syrup with maple flavoring. Cook with the skin on, but remove the skin from the salmon before serving.

SERVES 4

Serving size: 2 ounces salmon
Prep time: 15 minutes,
  plus 10 minutes to marinate
Cook time: 20 minutes

½ cup pure maple syrup
¼ cup gluten-free soy sauce
8 ounces salmon, cut into 2-ounce pieces

Substitution Tip: Try replacing the soy sauce with an equal amount of freshly squeezed orange juice and add 1 teaspoon of orange zest to the marinade.

1. Preheat the oven to 400°F.

2. In a small bowl, whisk together the maple syrup and soy sauce.

3. Add the salmon pieces and marinate for 10 minutes.

4. Remove the salmon pieces from the marinade and place them, skin-side down, on a baking sheet.

5. Bake in the preheated oven for 15 to 20 minutes until the salmon is opaque.

 PER SERVING CALORIES: 173; PROTEIN: 11G; TOTAL FAT: 4G; SATURATED FAT: 1G; CARBOHYDRATES: 27G; SUGAR: 23G; FIBER: 0G; SODIUM: 77MG

Baked Fish Sticks

DAIRY-FREE | GERD-FRIENDLY

These breaded fish sticks are baked, and low in fat. To make the fish sticks gluten-free, choose a gluten-free breadcrumb. Serve them with lemon wedges, or if you can eat dairy, use the Tartar Sauce (page 151) for dipping, or whisk some lemon zest and salt into a little bit of plain low-fat Greek yogurt for a simple dipping sauce.

SERVES 4
Serving size: 2 sticks
Prep time: 15 minutes
Cook time: 15 minutes

----

2 egg whites
1 teaspoon Dijon mustard
1 cup breadcrumbs
½ teaspoon sea salt
½ teaspoon lemon zest
8 ounces cod, skin removed and
    cut into 8 strips

Cooking Tip: You can easily make your own breadcrumbs. Put bread out on baking sheets on the counter over-night to dry it slightly. Then, cut the bread into cubes and pulse them in the food processor until they reach the desired consistency.

1. Preheat the oven to 450°F. Line a baking sheet with parchment.

2. In a small bowl, whisk together the egg whites and mustard.

3. In another small bowl, mix the breadcrumbs, salt, and zest.

4. Dip the fish pieces in the egg mixture and then into the breadcrumb mixture. Place the pieces on the prepared baking sheet.

5. Bake in the preheated oven until the fish is cooked through, about 12 minutes.

 PER SERVING CALORIES: 176; PROTEIN: 18G; TOTAL FAT: 2G; SATURATED FAT: 0G; CARBOHYDRATES: 20G; SUGAR: 2G; FIBER: 1G; SODIUM: 507MG

Chicken Meatballs in Broth

GLUTEN-FREE | DAIRY-FREE | LOW-CARB | LOW-SUGAR | GERD-FRIENDLY

These simple chicken meatballs in broth make a delicious meal. Cooking the meatballs and the spinach in broth keeps the meat and vegetables tender, and the dish is low in sugar and carbohydrates for people who are trying to manage their blood sugar.

SERVES 8
Serving size: 2 meatballs, 1 cup broth
Prep time: 15 minutes
Cook time: 20 minutes

———

4 ounces shiitake mushrooms,
   very finely chopped
1 pound ground chicken breast (skinless)
1 carrot, peeled and grated
½ teaspoon sea salt
½ teaspoon grated peeled fresh ginger
¼ teaspoon sesame oil
2 tablespoons chopped cilantro
¼ teaspoon lime zest
8 cups Poultry Stock (page 147)
2 cups baby spinach, stems trimmed

Cooking Tip: If you have a food processor, you can finely chop the mushrooms by pulsing them for 10 one-second pulses.

1. In a large bowl, combine the mushrooms, chicken, carrot, salt, ginger, sesame oil, cilantro, and zest. Form into 16 meatballs.

2. In a large pot, heat the stock over medium-high heat until it boils.

3. Drop in the meatballs. Boil, stirring occasionally, until the meatballs are completely cooked, about 15 minutes.

4. Stir in the spinach and cook for 2 minutes more.

5. Serve the meatballs with the broth and spinach spooned over them.

PER SERVING CALORIES: 190; PROTEIN: 37G; TOTAL FAT: 1G; SATURATED FAT: 0G; CARBOHYDRATES: 8G; SUGAR: 4G; FIBER: 1G; SODIUM: 676MG

Spaghetti Squash with Turkey-Tomato Sauce

GLUTEN-FREE | DAIRY-FREE | LOW-FODMAP | LOW-CARB
LOW-SUGAR | SIBO-FRIENDLY

Spaghetti squash makes a great low-carb alternative to pasta, so it's perfect for people seeking better blood sugar control. While this recipe calls for half a spaghetti squash, you can bake a whole squash and freeze the other half for another meal.

SERVES 8

Serving size: ½ squash, ½ sauce
Prep time: 15 minutes
Cook time: 45 minutes

———

½ spaghetti squash, seeds removed
2 tablespoons extra-virgin olive oil
1 pound ground turkey breast (skinless)
Basic Tomato Sauce (page 149)
2 tablespoons chopped fresh basil

Cooking Tip: You can also cook spaghetti squash in a slow cooker. To do so, prick the whole squash with a fork multiple times. Put it in a slow cooker with about ¼ cup of water. Cook on low for 6 to 8 hours, until tender.

1. Preheat the oven to 400°F. Line a baking sheet with parchment.

2. Put the squash, cut-side down on the baking sheet.

3. Bake for 30 to 45 minutes until the squash is tender.

4. While the squash cooks, prepare the sauce. In a large sauté pan, heat the olive oil on medium-high until it shimmers.

5. Add the turkey and cook for 5 to 7 minutes, crumbling with a spoon, until it is browned.

6. Stir in the tomato sauce and bring to a simmer.

7. Using a fork, run the tines across the squash to create strands.

8. Remove the sauce from the heat and stir in the basil. Serve the squash strands topped with the sauce.

 PER SERVING CALORIES: 232; PROTEIN: 19G; TOTAL FAT: 12G; SATURATED FAT: 2G; CARBOHYDRATES: 15G; SUGAR: 10G; FIBER: 3G; SODIUM: 222MG

Shrimp and Spinach Alfredo

This simple pasta dish features a low-fat Alfredo Sauce (page 156) that comes together very quickly. While the recipe calls for fettuccine, you can use any pasta shape you choose. Rotini pasta is another shape that works particularly well with creamy Alfredo sauce.

SERVES 4

Serving size: 2 ounces pasta,
 ½ cup sauce
Prep time: 15 minutes
Cook time: 15 minutes

———————

8 ounces fettuccine
1 tablespoon extra-virgin olive oil
3 scallions, green parts only, chopped
8 ounces baby shrimp
2 cups baby spinach, trimmed
½ teaspoon sea salt
Alfredo Sauce (page 156)
¼ cup low-fat Parmesan cheese (optional)

Substitution Tip: To add a pop of color, you can stir in ¼ cup of chopped roasted red peppers when you add the spinach.

1. Cook the fettuccine according to package directions. Set aside to drain in a colander.

2. In a large sauté pan, heat the olive oil on medium-high until it shimmers.

3. Add the scallions and cook, stirring occasionally, for 3 minutes.

4. Add the shrimp, spinach, and salt. Cook, stirring occasionally, until the spinach wilts and the shrimp is cooked, about 5 minutes.

5. Stir in the Alfredo sauce. Cook, stirring constantly for 1 to 2 minutes until the sauce is heated through.

6. Serve the sauce on top of the pasta sprinkled with the Parmesan cheese (if using).

PER SERVING CALORIES: 401; PROTEIN: 26G; TOTAL FAT: 14G; SATURATED FAT: 6G; CARBOHYDRATES: 43G; SUGAR: 7G; FIBER: 1G; SODIUM: 1015MG

Chicken Fingers with Country Gravy

Make a simple country gravy to dip these baked chicken fingers. It makes a delicious and quick meal that the whole family will enjoy, particularly when you serve it alongside steamed vegetables or mashed potatoes. It's a perfect weeknight meal for a busy family.

SERVES 4
Serving size: 2 ounces chicken and ¼ cup gravy
Prep time: 15 minutes
Cook time: 25 minutes

For the chicken fingers

2 eggs, beaten
1 tablespoon Dijon mustard
1 cup breadcrumbs
½ teaspoon dried thyme
½ teaspoon sea salt
8 ounces chicken breast tenders, cut into 1-ounce pieces

For the gravy

2 tablespoons extra-virgin olive oil
2 scallions green parts only, finely chopped
2 tablespoons flour
1 cup Poultry Stock (page 147)
1 cup nonfat milk
½ teaspoon sea salt
½ teaspoon dried thyme

Substitution Tip: You can replace the chicken tenders with turkey breast in this recipe, as well.

To make the chicken fingers

1. Preheat the oven to 425°F. Line a baking sheet with parchment.

2. In a small bowl, whisk together the eggs and mustard.

3. In another small bowl, combine the breadcrumbs, thyme, and salt.

4. Dip the chicken tenders into the egg mixture and then into the breadcrumb mixture, covering both sides of the meat. Place the pieces on the prepared baking sheet.

5. Bake in the preheated oven until the chicken is cooked and the breadcrumbs are golden, about 15 minutes.

To make the gravy

1. In a small saucepan, heat the olive oil on medium-high until it shimmers.

2. Add the scallions and cook, stirring occasionally, for 3 minutes.

3. Add the flour and cook, stirring constantly, for 1 minute.

4. Whisk in the stock, milk, salt, and thyme. Cook, stirring constantly, until thick, about 3 minutes more.

5. Serve the chicken fingers with the gravy spooned on top, or on the side for dipping.

PER SERVING CALORIES: 296; PROTEIN: 21G; TOTAL FAT: 11G; SATURATED FAT: 2G; CARBOHYDRATES: 27G; SUGAR: 5G; FIBER: 2G; SODIUM: 975MG

10

BROTHS, SAUCES & CONDIMENTS

Applesauce

GLUTEN-FREE | DAIRY-FREE

This simple applesauce is sweetened with pure maple syrup, giving it a warm maple flavor. It also has ginger, which is great for settling your stomach. Try it as a side dish, for breakfast, or add it to smoothies for additional nutrients and calories.

SERVES 8

Serving size: ½ cup
Prep time: 10 minutes
Cook time: 30 minutes

------

6 apples, peeled, cored, and cut
    into 1-inch pieces
1 tablespoon grated peeled fresh ginger
½ cup water or apple juice
Juice of ½ lemon, strained
½ teaspoon ground cinnamon
¼ cup pure maple syrup

Ingredient Tip: Using more than one type of apples results in a pleasingly complex-flavored sauce. Consider using 3 tart apples, such as Granny Smith, and 3 sweet-tart apples, such as Honeycrisp.

1. In a large pot, combine the apples, ginger, water or apple juice, lemon juice, and cinnamon. Bring the mixture to a boil over medium-high heat.

2. Reduce the heat to medium-low. Cover and simmer, stirring occasionally, until the apples are cooked through, 20 to 30 minutes.

3. Allow the apples to cool. Transfer them to a blender and blend on high for 1 minute.

4. Strain the applesauce through a large-holed colander, discarding any solids that remain in the colander.

5. Stir in the maple syrup.

 PER SERVING CALORIES: 107; PROTEIN: 1G; TOTAL FAT: 0G; SATURATED FAT: 0G; CARBOHYDRATES: 28G; SUGAR: 22G; FIBER: 4G; SODIUM: MG

Berry Sauce

GLUTEN-FREE | DAIRY-FREE

You can use berry sauce for a number of applications—from adding it to yogurt for a tasty breakfast to a dessert or ice cream topping. Berry sauce even tastes good when it tops fish or poultry. Make this ahead of time and keep it frozen in ice cube trays so you have single servings readily available to thaw.

SERVES 4

Serving size: 2 tablespoons
Prep time: 10 minutes
Cook time: 10 minutes

––––––––

2 cups mixed berries (fresh or frozen)
¼ cup of water
½ teaspoon ground cinnamon
3 drops liquid stevia

Ingredient Tip: For the most flavorful results, use fresh, seasonal, locally available berries.

1. Combine all of the ingredients in a large pot and bring to a simmer over medium-high heat.

2. Cook, stirring occasionally, until the berries are soft, about 10 minutes.

3. Transfer the mixture to a blender and blend on high for 30 seconds.

4. Strain the berry sauce through a colander, discarding the seeds and solids.

 PER SERVING CALORIES: 31; PROTEIN: 1G; TOTAL FAT: 0G; SATURATED FAT: 0G; CARBOHYDRATES: 8G; SUGAR: 4G; FIBER: 2G; SODIUM: 1MG

Carob Sauce

GLUTEN-FREE

While many people with gastroparesis can't tolerate chocolate, they can tolerate carob, so this tasty sauce makes a great substitute. Serve it on nonfat ice cream or frozen yogurt, or drizzle it over cooked fruits for a delicious dessert. It also works well as a base for carob hot cocoa.

SERVES 4
Serving size: 2 tablespoons
Prep time: 5 minutes
Cook time: 5 minutes

———————

¼ cup carob powder
1 tablespoon melted butter
¼ cup nonfat milk
2 tablespoons water
¼ cup sugar

Substitution Tip: For carob–peanut butter sauce, add 1 tablespoon of peanut butter.

1. In a medium pot, combine all of the ingredients.

2. Heat on medium-high, stirring constantly, until smooth, 3 to 5 minutes.

3. Stir in the maple syrup.

 PER SERVING CALORIES: 154; PROTEIN: 2G; TOTAL FAT: 7G; SATURATED FAT: 6G; CARBOHYDRATES: 21G; SUGAR: 18G; FIBER: 1G; SODIUM: 44MG

Vegetable Stock

GLUTEN-FREE | DAIRY-FREE | LOW-FODMAP | LOW-CARB
LOW-SUGAR | SIBO-FRIENDLY | GERD-FRIENDLY

I'm a big fan of preparing all kinds of stocks in your slow cooker, where you just have to dump in the ingredients and forget all about them. This stock uses mushrooms to get a heartier, more savory flavor from the other ingredients. Freeze the stock in 1-cup servings so you always have some available.

YIELD: 8 CUPS
Prep time: 10 minutes
Cook time: 12 to 24 hours

———————

4 carrots, peeled and cut into pieces
2 celery stalks, peeled and cut
    into pieces
8 scallions, green parts only,
    roughly chopped
8 ounces mushrooms
8 cups water
1 teaspoon sea salt
2 sprigs fresh thyme

Cooking Tip: One of my favorite stock-making tips is to save vegetable trimmings in a resealable plastic bag in the freezer. Then, when it comes time to make stock, I dump in my vegetable trimmings and make a stock from them.

1. Combine all of the ingredients in the slow cooker.

2. Cover and cook on low for 12 to 24 hours. The longer the cook time, the more flavorful the stock will be.

3. Strain the stock through a fine-meshed sieve.

PER SERVING CALORIES: 15; PROTEIN: 0G; TOTAL FAT: 0G; SATURATED FAT: 0G; CARBOHYDRATES: 3G; SUGAR: 3G; FIBER: 0G; SODIUM: 570MG

Fish Stock

GLUTEN-FREE | DAIRY-FREE | LOW-FODMAP | LOW-CARB
LOW-SUGAR | SIBO-FRIENDLY | GERD-FRIENDLY

Seafood scraps make great fish stock. So whenever you peel shrimp, shell crab or lobster, or cut the heads off fish, save them in a resealable plastic bag in the freezer so they're ready when you want to make stock. Make this in the slow cooker so it's easy and hands-off.

YIELD: 8 CUPS
Prep time: 15 minutes
Cook time: 12 hours

––––––––

6 cups seafood trimmings, such as
    shrimp shells and tails, crab shells,
    and fish heads
8 scallions, green parts only
2 carrots, peeled and roughly chopped
2 stalks fennel, peeled and
    roughly chopped
2 sprigs fresh tarragon
1 teaspoon sea salt
8 cups water

Cooking Tip: You can also make this recipe on the stovetop, simmering in a large pot for 3 to 4 hours.

1. Combine all of the ingredients in a slow cooker.

2. Simmer on low for 12 hours.

3. Strain through a fine-mesh sieve, discarding any solids.

PER SERVING CALORIES: 40; PROTEIN: 5G; TOTAL FAT: 2G; SATURATED FAT: 0G; CARBOHYDRATES: 0G; SUGAR: 0G; FIBER: 0G; SODIUM: 363MG

Poultry Stock

GLUTEN-FREE | DAIRY-FREE | LOW-FODMAP | LOW-CARB
LOW-SUGAR | SIBO-FRIENDLY | GERD-FRIENDLY

Stock is a great way to use up otherwise un-useable poultry parts, such as necks, backs, or carcasses. You can use any type of chicken, turkey, or duck bones—either cooked or uncooked—to flavor the stock. While this calls for a slow cooker, you can also make the stock on the stovetop, simmering on low for 5 to 6 hours.

YIELD: 8 CUPS
Serving size: 1 cup
Prep time: 15 minutes,
  plus overnight to chill
Cook time: 12 to 24 hours

———————

3 pounds poultry pieces or bones
8 scallions, green parts only
2 carrots, peeled and roughly chopped
2 sprigs fresh rosemary
1 teaspoon sea salt
8 cups water

*Substitution Tip: Add slices of fresh
ginger to make a fragrant, spicier broth.*

1. Combine all of the ingredients in a slow cooker.

2. Simmer on low for 12 to 24 hours.

3. Strain through a fine-meshed sieve, discarding the solids.

4. Refrigerate the stock overnight. In the morning, skim away any fat that has collected on the top of the broth.

PER SERVING CALORIES: 20; PROTEIN: 4G; TOTAL FAT: 0G; SATURATED FAT: 0G; CARBOHYDRATES: 1G; SUGAR: 1G; FIBER: 0G; SODIUM: 130MG

Beef Stock

GLUTEN-FREE | DAIRY-FREE | LOW-CARB | LOW-SUGAR
SIBO-FRIENDLY | GERD-FRIENDLY

This beef stock is made even richer with the addition of dried mushrooms. It makes a great soup base, or use it to cook grains such as rice to give them a beefier flavor. Simmering the bones adds plenty of nutrients, particularly minerals, and the parsley adds additional iron. Because you skim the fat away before using, it's also a low-fat food.

YIELD: 8 CUPS

Prep time: 15 minutes,
 plus overnight to chill

Cook time: 24 hours

———

4 pounds beef bones

2 ounces dried porcini mushrooms

8 scallions, green parts only

2 carrots, peeled and roughly chopped

1 celery stalk, peeled and
 roughly chopped

1 sprig fresh rosemary

1 sprig fresh thyme

¼ cup chopped fresh parsley

1 teaspoon sea salt

8 cups water

Substitution Tip: To extract even more minerals from the bones to make the broth more nutritious, add a table-spoon of raw apple cider vinegar along with the other ingredients.

1. Combine all of the ingredients in a slow cooker.

2. Simmer on low for 24 hours.

3. Strain through a fine-meshed sieve, discarding the solids.

4. Refrigerate overnight. In the morning, skim away any fat that has collected on the top of the broth and discard.

 PER SERVING CALORIES: 15; PROTEIN: 4G; TOTAL FAT: 0G; SATURATED FAT: 0G; CARBOHYDRATES: 0G; SUGAR: 0G; FIBER: 0G; SODIUM: 440MG

Basic Tomato Sauce

GLUTEN-FREE | DAIRY-FREE

Starchy carrots thicken this simple tomato sauce, which is really easy to make. It serves as an excellent pasta topper, or you can use it on top of fish or poultry for a meal. This freezes well, so make a big batch and freeze it in 1-cup servings for easy use in recipes.

SERVES 8
Serving size: 1 cup
Prep time: 10 minutes
Cook time: 30 minutes

2 tablespoons extra-virgin olive oil

8 scallions, green parts only, chopped

6 cups strained tomato juice

1 pound baby carrots, peeled
   and chopped

1 teaspoon dried oregano

½ teaspoon sea salt

1 tablespoon chopped fresh
   flat-leaf parsley

2 tablespoons chopped fresh basil

Cooking Tip: To make the sauce smoother, you can strain it through a fine-meshed sieve before using. Use a spoon to gently press the sauce through the sieve.

1. In a large pot, heat the olive oil on medium-high until it shimmers.

2. Add the scallions and cook, stirring occasionally, until soft, 3 to 4 minutes.

3. Add the tomato juice, baby carrots, oregano, and salt. Simmer, stirring occasionally, until the carrots are soft, about 30 minutes.

4. Transfer the tomato sauce and carrots to a blender. Add the parsley and basil. Blend until smooth, 1 to 2 minutes.

 PER SERVING CALORIES: 87; PROTEIN: 2G; TOTAL FAT: 4G; SATURATED FAT: 1G; CARBOHYDRATES: 14G; SUGAR: 10G; FIBER: 3G; SODIUM: 654MG

Easy Barbecue Sauce

GLUTEN-FREE | DAIRY-FREE

Make your own barbecue sauce from tomato sauce, herbs, and spices. For a smoky flavor, you'll need some liquid smoke, which you can find in the spice aisle of your grocery store. Just remember, a little goes a very long way, so be judicious.

SERVES 8

Serving size: 2 tablespoons
Prep time: 5 minutes
Cook time: 10 minutes

---

1 tablespoon extra-virgin olive oil
4 scallions, green parts only,
    finely chopped
¾ cup tomato sauce
¼ teaspoon liquid smoke
2 tablespoons apple cider vinegar
1 tablespoon honey
1 tablespoon dark brown sugar
½ teaspoon sea salt
¼ teaspoon ground nutmeg
½ teaspoon ground cumin
1 teaspoon orange zest

1. In a small saucepan, heat the olive oil on medium-high heat until it shimmers.

2. Add the scallions and cook, stirring frequently, for 3 minutes.

3. Stir in the tomato sauce, liquid smoke, vinegar, honey, brown sugar, salt, nutmeg, cumin, and zest. Bring to a boil and reduce the heat to medium-low.

4. Simmer, stirring frequently, for 5 minutes.

Substitution Tip: This is a great recipe to customize based on your individual tastes and the herbs and spices you can tolerate, which might include garlic powder, chili powder, and smoked paprika. To make this sauce vegan, substitute maple syrup for the honey.

PER SERVING CALORIES: 37; PROTEIN: 1G; TOTAL FAT: 2G; SATURATED FAT: 0G; CARBOHYDRATES: 5G; SUGAR: 4G; FIBER: 1G; SODIUM: 239MG

Tartar Sauce

GLUTEN-FREE

This is a fat-free version of tartar sauce that you can use to dip fish, sweet potato fries, or other snack foods. It uses nonfat, plain Greek yogurt as its base, which has a nice tang to it. Lemon zest adds a little more tang, which nicely complements the chopped pickle.

SERVES 4

Serving size: 2 tablespoons
Prep time: 5 minutes
Cook time: None

½ cup nonfat, plain Greek yogurt
1 small dill pickle, finely chopped
1 teaspoon chopped fresh dill
¼ teaspoon lemon zest
1 teaspoon apple cider vinegar
½ teaspoon sea salt

Substitution Tip: To make this sauce dairy free, replace the yogurt with fat-free mayonnaise.

Combine all of the ingredients in a small bowl and stir well. Serve immediately, or store in the refrigerator for up to three days.

 PER SERVING CALORIES: 3; PROTEIN: 0G; TOTAL FAT: 0G; SATURATED FAT: 0G; CARBOHYDRATES: 0G; SUGAR: 0G; FIBER: 0G; SODIUM: 403MG

Mock Sour Cream

GLUTEN-FREE

Sour cream is pretty high in fat, but this low-fat version approximates the flavor and texture without chemicals that you might find in other nonfat sour cream substitutes. It comes together very quickly and has a wonderful, tangy flavor.

SERVES 8

Serving size: 2 tablespoons
Prep time: 5 minutes
Cook time: None

———————

1 cup low-fat or nonfat cottage cheese
2 tablespoons nonfat milk
1 scallion, green part only,
    finely minced (optional)
Juice of ½ lemon, strained
Pinch sea salt

Substitution Tip: You can also use nonfat plain yogurt in place of the cottage cheese.

Combine all of the ingredients in a blender or food processor and process until smooth.

 PER SERVING CALORIES: 3; PROTEIN: 0G; TOTAL FAT: 0G; SATURATED FAT: 0G; CARBOHYDRATES: 0G; SUGAR: 0G; FIBER: 0G; SODIUM: 90MG

Vegan Mayonnaise

GLUTEN-FREE | DAIRY-FREE

This is a really easy low-fat, vegan replacement for mayonnaise, which tends to be high in fat and contains eggs. Use it as a sandwich spread or as a base for easy chicken salad, potato salad, or similar recipes. It uses silken tofu and has a tangy flavor.

SERVES 8
Serving size: 2 tablespoons
Prep time: 5 minutes
Cook time: None

———————

1 cup silken tofu
1 tablespoon extra-virgin olive oil
Juice of ½ lemon, strained
1 teaspoon Dijon mustard
1 drop liquid stevia
½ teaspoon sea salt

Cooking Tip: This will store in the refrigerator, tightly sealed, for up to a week.

Combine all of the ingredients in a blender or food processor and process until smooth.

 PER SERVING CALORIES: 23; PROTEIN: 1G; TOTAL FAT: 2G; SATURATED FAT: 0G; CARBOHYDRATES: 0G; SUGAR: 0G; FIBER: 0G; SODIUM: 128MG

Vegetarian Gravy

GLUTEN-FREE | DAIRY-FREE | LOW-FODMAP | LOW-CARB
LOW-SUGAR | SIBO-FRIENDLY | GERD-FRIENDLY

Sometimes, you just want gravy. This is a really easy way to make a vegetarian gravy that's thick, rich, low in fat, and packed with nutrients. Use it to top purées, or serve it alongside meat, fish, or poultry to add flavor and richness.

SERVES 16
Serving size: ¼ cup
Prep time: 15 minutes
Cook time: 25 minutes

2 tablespoons extra-virgin olive oil
4 scallions, green parts only, chopped
3 cups Vegetable Stock (page 145)
2 large carrots, peeled and chopped
4 ounces mushrooms, chopped
1 teaspoon dried thyme
½ teaspoon sea salt

Substitution Tip: For an even more savory gravy, soak 2 ounces of dried mushrooms in the hot broth for 1 to 2 hours before making the gravy.

1. In a medium pot, heat the olive oil on medium-high until it shimmers.

2. Add the scallions and cook, stirring occasionally, until soft, 3 to 4 minutes.

3. Add the vegetable stock, carrots, mushrooms, thyme, and salt. Bring the mixture to a boil. Reduce the heat to medium and simmer until the carrots are very soft, about 20 minutes.

4. Transfer the mixture to a blender. Blend on high until smooth, about 1 minute.

 PER SERVING CALORIES: 24; PROTEIN: 0G; TOTAL FAT: 2G; SATURATED FAT: 0G; CARBOHYDRATES: 2G; SUGAR: 1G; FIBER: 0G; SODIUM: 173MG

Meat Gravy

LOW-FODMAP | LOW-CARB | LOW-SUGAR | SIBO-FRIENDLY | GERD-FRIENDLY

This hearty meat gravy uses flour as a thickener, although it remains relatively low in fat due to the small amount of olive oil used. You can use any type of meat stock (beef or poultry) to make this gravy, which serves as a wonderful topping for turkey or chicken breast.

SERVES 8
Serving size: ¼ cup
Prep time: 5 minutes
Cook time: 10 minutes

————

2 tablespoons unsalted butter
2 scallions, green parts only,
    finely chopped
¼ cup water
2 tablespoons flour
2 cups Beef Stock (page 148)
    or Poultry Stock (page 147)
½ teaspoon dried thyme
½ teaspoon sea salt

Substitution Tip: To make this gluten-free, use rice flour in place of wheat flour.

1. In a medium pan, heat the unsalted butter on medium-high until it bubbles.

2. Add the scallions and cook, stirring frequently, until soft, about 2 minutes.

3. Whisk together the water and flour in a glass measuring cup until there are no lumps.

4. Slowly whisk in the flour-water mixture to avoid lumps, and cook, stirring constantly, for 1 minute.

5. Add the stock, thyme, and salt. Bring the gravy to a simmer, stirring constantly, until the gravy thickens.

 PER SERVING CALORIES: 38; PROTEIN: 1G; TOTAL FAT: 3G; SATURATED FAT: 2G; CARBOHYDRATES: 2G; SUGAR: 0G; FIBER: 0G; SODIUM: 248MG

Alfredo Sauce

This simple white sauce is typically high in fat. Using lower fat ingredients, however, yields the same flavor as a typical Alfredo sauce, but with less fat. It's also high in calcium and other minerals, and it makes a good pasta sauce or topping for fish or poultry.

SERVES 8

Serving size: ¼ cup

Prep time: 15 minutes

Cook time: 10 minutes

———————

2 tablespoons unsalted butter

2 tablespoons flour

2 cups nonfat milk

¼ cup low-fat Parmesan cheese

¼ teaspoon sea salt

Pinch ground nutmeg

Substitution Tip: To make this a simple, dairy-free and gluten-free white sauce, replace the butter with olive oil, the flour with sweet rice flour, and the milk with almond milk. Omit the Parmesan cheese.

1. In a medium saucepan, heat the butter on medium-high until it bubbles.

2. Add the flour and cook, whisking constantly, for 1 minute until flour and butter are completely incorporated and a slight nutty flavor rises from the pan.

3. Whisk in the milk and bring to a simmer, whisking constantly for 2 to 3 minutes, until the sauce thickens and there are no lumps.

4. Stir in the cheese, salt, and nutmeg.

 PER SERVING CALORIES: 67; PROTEIN: 3G; TOTAL FAT: 4G; SATURATED FAT: 2G; CARBOHYDRATES: 5G; SUGAR: 3G; FIBER: 0G; SODIUM: 144MG

Warm Gingered Poultry Broth

GLUTEN-FREE | DAIRY-FREE | LOW-CARB

Ginger works really well to soothe an upset stomach, so sipping on a cup of gingered broth may be just the ticket when you are experiencing flare-ups. While chicken, turkey, or duck broth go best with the ginger flavor, you can also try it with beef or fish broth, or any broth you have on hand.

SERVES 1
Serving size: 1 cup
Prep time: 5 minutes
Cook time: 10 minutes

———————

1¼ cup Poultry Stock (page 147)
2 slices peeled fresh ginger
Pinch salt

Ingredient Tip: To make an entire pot of gingered broth, add four or five slices of ginger when you are making any of the stock recipes found in this chapter.

1. In a small saucepan, combine the broth, ginger, and salt.

2. Simmer on medium for 10 minutes, stirring occasionally.

3. Remove the ginger slices and pour into a mug.

 PER SERVING CALORIES: 26; PROTEIN: 4G; TOTAL FAT: 0G; SATURATED FAT: 0G; CARBOHYDRATES: 2G; SUGAR: 1G; FIBER: 0G; SODIUM: 286MG

11
DESSERT & SWEETS

Orange Dreamsicle Ice Pops

GLUTEN-FREE

You don't need ice pop molds to make these creamy orange-vanilla flavored pops. Instead, you can make them in paper cups. Place a piece of foil over the filled cups and insert an ice pop stick. The foil will hold the sticks in place. Then, when you're ready to eat them, you can peel away the foil and the cup.

SERVES 4

Serving size: 1 pop

Prep time: 5 minutes,
   plus overnight to freeze

Cook time: None

———

2 cups orange juice, strained

1 cup nonfat plain yogurt

½ teaspoon alcohol-free vanilla extract

2 teaspoons honey

Substitution Tip: You can use any flavor of strained juice in place of the orange juice in these pops. To make them dairy-free, use a dairy-free cultured product, such as plain almond yogurt.

1. In a blender, combine all of the ingredients and process for 30 seconds.

2. Pour the mixture into ice pop molds or paper cups.

3. Freeze overnight.

PER SERVING CALORIES: 285; PROTEIN: 7G; TOTAL FAT: 0G; SATURATED FAT: 0G; CARBOHYDRATES: 64G; SUGAR: 57G; FIBER: 0G; SODIUM: 60MG

Coconut-Berry Ice Pops

GLUTEN-FREE | DAIRY-FREE

These ice pops don't take a lot of work, but they do take a bit of patience if you want to make them in layers. If you lack patience, you can just blend the coconut milk and berry sauce together instead of layering them. Either way, you get a sweet, creamy, frozen treat.

SERVES 4
Serving size: 1 pop
Prep time: 5 minutes,
  plus 6 to 8 hours to freeze
Cook time: 5 minutes

———

2 cups light coconut milk
2 tablespoons honey
1 recipe Berry Sauce (page 143)

Substitution Tip: Want these available sooner? Blend the berry sauce and coconut milk mixture in a blender and pour it into the ice pop molds.

1. In a small saucepan, heat the coconut milk and honey, stirring constantly, until the honey is completely dissolved. Cool completely.

2. In 4 ice pop molds or paper cups, add a small layer of the coconut milk mixture. Insert sticks and freeze until solid, 3 to 4 hours.

3. Add a layer of the berry sauce and freeze again for 1 to 2 hours until solid.

4. Add another layer of the coconut milk mixture and freeze for 1 to 2 hours.

5. Finish with a final layer of the berry sauce. Freeze for 1 to 2 hours.

 PER SERVING CALORIES: 130; PROTEIN: 2G; TOTAL FAT: 6G; SATURATED FAT: 6G; CARBOHYDRATES: 21 G; SUGAR: 13G; FIBER: 2G; SODIUM: 31MG

Cranberry Granita

GLUTEN-FREE | DAIRY-FREE

This simple frozen dessert doesn't take much time to make, although you'll need to freeze it overnight, scraping the frozen juice into ice crystals with a fork. The result is a nutrient-rich and flavorful dessert.

SERVES 8
Serving size: ½ cup
Prep time: 15 minutes,
   plus 8 to 10 hours to freeze
Cook time: 7 minutes

———

2 cups water
1½ cups cranberries
Zest of 1 orange
½ cup honey

Substitution Tip: You can substitute blackberries, blueberries, or raspberries for the cranberries in this granita.

1. In a small saucepan, heat the water, cranberries, zest, and honey for 5 to 7 minutes until the cranberries begin to pop.

2. Transfer the mixture to a blender and process until smooth.

3. Hold a fine-mesh sieve over a 9-by-13-inch baking pan and pour the purée through it, allowing the juices to drip into the pan and discarding the solids.

4. Pour the mixture into a shallow dish or pan. Freeze for 2 hours.

5. Scrape the granita with a fork and refreeze for 2 to 8 hours longer.

6. Scrape with a fork again and serve.

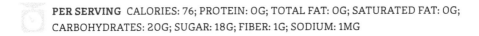 **PER SERVING** CALORIES: 76; PROTEIN: 0G; TOTAL FAT: 0G; SATURATED FAT: 0G; CARBOHYDRATES: 20G; SUGAR: 18G; FIBER: 1G; SODIUM: 1MG

Ginger-Pear Granita

GLUTEN-FREE | DAIRY-FREE | LOW-FODMAP

Granita makes a refreshing frozen dessert. With its icy texture, it offers vivid fruit flavors without totally filling you up. With its hint of ginger, this ginger-pear sorbet may also just soothe an upset stomach while providing a little bit of hydration.

SERVES 4

Serving size: ½ cup

Prep time: 15 minutes,
   plus 8 to 10 hours to freeze

Cook time: 10 minutes

———

3 pears, peeled, cored, and cut
   into small pieces

¼ cup water

12 ounces ginger ale

Substitution Tip: You can replace the pears with 1 cup of Applesauce (page 142) for a ginger-apple sorbet.

1. In a small saucepan, cook the pears in the water on medium-high heat, stirring frequently, until the pears are soft, about 10 minutes. Add more water if needed during cooking.

2. In a blender or food processor, purée the pears, along with their cooking liquid, and the ginger ale.

3. Pour the mixture into a shallow dish or pan. Freeze for 2 hours.

4. Scrape the granita with a fork and re-freeze for 2 to 8 hours longer.

5. Scrape with a fork again and serve.

 PER SERVING CALORIES: 120; PROTEIN: 1G; TOTAL FAT: 0G; SATURATED FAT: 0G; CARBOHYDRATES: 31G; SUGAR: 23G; FIBER: 5G; SODIUM: 8MG

Anise and Honey Poached Pears

GLUTEN-FREE | DAIRY-FREE

Poached pears make a tasty and healthy dessert. You can serve them warm or cold, or use them to top your favorite ice cream. You can use any sweet spices you wish, such as cinnamon or nutmeg. This version calls for anise, giving the pears a subtle licorice flavor.

SERVES 4
Serving size: ½ pear
Prep time: 5 minutes
Cook time: 30 minutes

———————

2 cups apple juice
1 teaspoon anise seeds
¼ cup honey
2 cloves
2 pears, peeled, cored, and halved

Cooking Tip: You can eat the poached pears warm, or keep them in the refrigerator in the poaching liquid for 2 to 3 days. If you like, you can reheat them before serving, or serve them chilled.

1. In a medium pot, bring the juice, anise, honey, and cloves to a simmer.

2. Add the pears. Cover and cook for 30 minutes. Serve warm or chilled, with or without the poaching liquid.

PER SERVING CALORIES: 185; PROTEIN: 1G; TOTAL FAT: 0G; SATURATED FAT: 0G; CARBOHYDRATES: 48G; SUGAR: 41G; FIBER: 4G; SODIUM: 6MG

Coconut Flan

GLUTEN-FREE | DAIRY-FREE | GERD-FRIENDLY

To make this custard, you need to temper the eggs before adding them to hot ingredients so they don't completely cook. Many people are tempted to skip this step, but it is an important part of making custard so you don't wind up with scrambled eggs in your dessert.

SERVES 4

Serving size: 1 ramekin
Prep time: 15 minutes
Cook time: 45 minutes

½ cup raw honey
4 eggs, beaten
1 (14-ounce) can light coconut milk
¼ cup honey
Pinch sea salt
1 teaspoon alcohol-free vanilla extract

Cooking Tip: This recipe calls for you to bake the custards in a water bath, which makes the cooking gentler. Use boiling water in the water bath, and be careful not to get any of the water into the ramekins.

1. Preheat the oven to 350°F.

2. In a small saucepan, heat the raw honey over medium-high heat, stirring occasionally, until it turns golden brown, about 5 minutes.

3. Pour the honey into the bottom of 4 ramekins.

4. In a small bowl, whisk the eggs until they are well beaten.

5. In a medium saucepan, bring the coconut milk, honey, salt, and vanilla to a simmer, stirring constantly.

6. Remove the pan from the heat and add the warm mixture to the eggs, a teaspoon at a time, stirring constantly, until you've added 2 to 3 tablespoons.

7. Add the egg mixture very slowly into the hot coconut milk in a thin stream, stirring constantly.

8. Pour the mixture into 4 ramekins. Put the ramekins in a baking pan and pour boiling water around the ramekins so that it comes about halfway up the sides of the ramekins.

9. Bake until the custards are set, about 40 minutes.

10. Remove from the oven and let cool completely at room temperature. Refrigerate, covered, for 3 hours. Invert onto small dishes and serve.

PER SERVING CALORIES: 315; PROTEIN: 7G; TOTAL FAT: 9G; SATURATED FAT: 6G; CARBOHYDRATES: 57G; SUGAR: 53G; FIBER: 0G; SODIUM: 148MG

Maple Custard

GLUTEN-FREE | DAIRY-FREE

This simple custard is high in protein due to the eggs, and is creamy and delicious. Use pure maple syrup, which gives the custard and delicious warm, sweet taste. Be sure to cook the ramekins in a water bath to keep the custard from burning.

SERVES 4
Serving size: 1 ramekin
Prep time: 15 minutes
Cook time: 45 minutes

———————

4 eggs, beaten
2 cups Almond Milk (page 57)
¼ cup pure maple syrup
½ teaspoon orange zest

Cooking Tip: You can perform the spoon test to see if the custard is thick enough. While you boil the custard in step 6, coat the back of a metal spoon with the custard and run your finger along the center of the spoon. If the track from your finger stays, the custard is thick enough. Do this carefully, because the custard will be hot.

1. Preheat the oven to 350°F.

2. In a small bowl, beat the eggs.

3. In a medium pot, heat the almond milk, maple syrup, and zest over medium-high heat until it boils, stirring constantly.

4. Stirring constantly, add the hot milk mixture to the beaten eggs, about a teaspoon at a time, until you've added 2 to 3 tablespoons of milk.

5. Stirring constantly, slowly add the egg mixture to the hot milk mixture.

6. Stirring constantly, bring the mixture to a boil, cooking until it thickens slightly.

7. Pour the mixture into 4 ramekins, and place the ramekins in a baking pan. Pour boiling water into the baking pan until it reaches halfway up the sides of the ramekins.

8. Bake in the water bath until the custards are set, about 40 minutes.

9. Cool completely before serving.

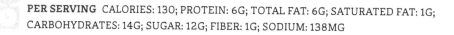

PER SERVING CALORIES: 130; PROTEIN: 6G; TOTAL FAT: 6G; SATURATED FAT: 1G; CARBOHYDRATES: 14G; SUGAR: 12G; FIBER: 1G; SODIUM: 138MG

Vanilla Pudding

GLUTEN-FREE | DAIRY-FREE | LOW-FODMAP | LOW-CARB
LOW-SUGAR | SIBO-FRIENDLY | GERD-FRIENDLY

This pudding uses arrowroot powder in place of cornstarch to thicken it. You can find arrowroot powder at health food stores or online. It is a great non-corn thickener that is slightly lower in carbohydrates than cornstarch or other thickeners.

SERVES 4

Serving size: ½ cup

Prep time: 10 minutes,
  plus 2 hours to chill

Cook time: 10 minutes

---

2 cups Almond Milk (page 57)

¼ cup arrowroot powder

6 drops liquid stevia

2 teaspoons alcohol-free vanilla extract

Substitution Tip: Substitute almond extract for the vanilla to make almond-flavored pudding.

1. In a small pot, whisk together the almond milk, arrowroot, stevia, and vanilla.

2. Put the pot on the stove and heat over medium heat, stirring constantly, until the mixture thickens, 4 to 5 minutes.

3. Remove the pot from the heat. Pour the mixture into individual ramekins and refrigerate until cooled, about 2 hours.

PER SERVING CALORIES: 56; PROTEIN: 1G; TOTAL FAT: 1G; SATURATED FAT: 0G; CARBOHYDRATES: 9G; SUGAR: 0G; FIBER: 1G; SODIUM: 75MG

Ice Cream with Mixed Berry Sauce

GLUTEN-FREE

Use frozen mixed berries to make this sauce, and select either low-fat vanilla ice cream or low-fat vanilla frozen yogurt. You can also make this with a mixture of any berries that you'd like to change the flavor profiles.

SERVES 4

Serving size: ½ cup ice cream,
  plus 2 tablespoons berry sauce
Prep time: 5 minutes
Cook time: 5 minutes

———————

2 cups frozen mixed berries
½ cup water
¼ teaspoon ground cinnamon
¼ cup honey
2 cups low-fat vanilla ice cream
  or frozen yogurt

Cooking Tip: If you don't have a good blender, you can also use a stick blender, also known as an immersion blender, to purée this sauce and other foods.

1. In a small saucepan, combine the berries, water, cinnamon, and honey.

2. Bring the mixture to a boil, stirring occasionally.

3. Pour the mixture into a blender and blend until smooth.

4. Pour the blended berries through a fine-mesh sieve, discarding any seeds and solids that remain.

5. Serve the ice cream topped with the berry sauce.

 PER SERVING CALORIES: 249; PROTEIN: 3G; TOTAL FAT: 8G; SATURATED FAT: 5G; CARBOHYDRATES: 43G; SUGAR: 38G; FIBER: 3G; SODIUM: 58MG

Ashley's Carob Pudding

GLUTEN-FREE | DAIRY-FREE | LOW-FODMAP | SIBO-FRIENDLY | GERD-FRIENDLY

Ashley Jenkins is a college student who was diagnosed with gastroparesis in 2011. She shares her story and tips for people suffering from gastroparesis in Appendix B: Stories from the Front Line *on page 174. Since chocolate is difficult for many people with gastroparesis, Ashley replaces it with carob powder, which you should be able to find at your local health food store.*

SERVES 4
Serving size: ½ cup
Prep time: 10 minutes
Cook time: 5 minutes

———————

¼ cup sugar
4 tablespoons carob powder
5 tablespoons arrowroot powder
2 cups Rice Milk (page 56), divided
1 teaspoon alcohol-free vanilla extract

Ashley's Tips: Allow up to 20 minutes to make. Keep a close eye on the pudding as it cooks; it thickens more quickly than you would expect. You can find more recipes by checking out my Facebook group (see page 193).

1. In a medium saucepan, stir together the sugar, carob, and arrowroot.

2. Add ½ cup rice milk and stir until the mixture is smooth.

3. Add the remaining 1½ cups of rice milk and cook for 3 to 5 minutes over medium heat until the mixture thickens and begins to boil.

4. Stir in the vanilla and remove the pot from the heat.

5. Let the mixture cool down before pouring into 4 small ramekins.

6. Refrigerate until ready to serve.

 PER SERVING CALORIES: 193; PROTEIN: 2G; TOTAL FAT: 5G; SATURATED FAT: 4G; CARBOHYDRATES: 36G; SUGAR: 18G; FIBER: 4G; SODIUM: 83MG

WHAT TO EXPECT
AT THE DOCTOR'S OFFICE

Obtaining a diagnosis of gastroparesis may take some time and several doctor's visits. Because gastroparesis symptoms are so similar to a number of gastrointestinal conditions, your doctor may require multiple tests to obtain an accurate diagnosis.

At Your First Visit

One of the best ways you can help your doctor reach an accurate diagnosis is by providing them with as much information as you can. When you first visit the doctor:

- Bring a diary of foods and symptoms so you can show your doctor when your symptoms are most likely to occur.

- Provide your doctor with a list of medications you currently take and any surgical procedures you have recently had.

- When you make the appointment, ask if there are any special instructions you need to follow before you meet with the doctor.

For many people, their first visit to a doctor for their condition is to a primary care specialist, such as an internist or family practitioner. At that appointment, you can expect to talk with your doctor, have your vitals measured, and undergo a physical examination. Your doctor may also order labs, such as blood tests, to rule out other conditions. After gathering as much information as possible, your doctor will likely refer you to a specialist, such as a gastroenterologist, for further diagnosis.

Tests

The Mayo Clinic notes that doctors may use multiple tests to diagnose gastroparesis.

UPPER GI ENDOSCOPY

One of the most common examinations for gastrointestinal conditions is the upper gastrointestinal tract endoscopy, or upper GI. During an upper GI, your doctor will insert a small camera on a thin, flexible tube into your alimentary canal via your mouth to look at the lining of your esophagus, stomach, and duodenum. To prepare for the procedure, your doctor will likely instruct you to take nothing by mouth after midnight the night before.

The day of the procedure, you will likely receive sedation and a topical local anesthetic for your throat. If you do receive sedation, it will likely be injected intravenously just prior to the procedure. (The anesthesia and/or sedation minimizes the gag reflex.) Then, you will lie on your side and your doctor will insert a mouthpiece through which the endoscope is then inserted. You will be required to swallow the tube/camera. Once the tube enters your alimentary canal, the doctor will likely puff a little air through the tube into your stomach to inflate it. The procedure will likely last about 10 to 15 minutes, and you may still feel the urge to gag, despite anesthesia. Breathe normally and try to resist the urge as much as possible.

If you have had sedation for the endoscopy, you'll need to remain in a recovery area for about an hour. After the test, you can discuss next steps with your doctor. If you've had IV sedation, refrain from operating heavy machinery or driving for at least 24 hours.

UPPER GI SERIES

Your doctor may also recommend that you get an upper GI series, which is a series of x-ray and fluoroscope images completed after you swallow barium, a radiocontrast medium. This chalky substance coats your GI tract and helps the doctors see exactly what's going on in the images. The purpose of this series is to observe stomach contractions to examine your upper digestive system and to check for other issues, such as scarring or blockages that might be contributing to your symptoms.

Before the appointment, your doctor may advise you not to eat, drink, or chew gum for about eight hours pre-procedure in order to clear your upper gastrointestinal tract. At the appointment, you will drink the barium. After consuming the barium, you will lie on an x-ray table and the technician or doctor will take images as the barium moves through the alimentary canal. This may take two hours or longer to complete, depending on how quickly the barium moves through your gastrointestinal tract.

While the barium is a little unpalatable, the series itself is painless. After the study you may experience some brief nausea, bloating, or gas, which should pass quickly.

OTHER IMAGING TESTS

Your doctor may also recommend CT or MRI scans of the gastrointestinal tract to rule out any intestinal blockages. During these tests, you will remove your clothes and any jewelry, and put on a gown. Then, you will lie on a table in either a tube or a machine while the machine takes images. These can be noisy, but they are noninvasive and painless.

GASTRIC EMPTYING STUDY

This test shows how quickly your stomach empties itself of food. Before the test, your doctor will instruct you not to take anything by mouth for about six to eight hours. At the doctor's office or imaging center, you will be given food that contains radionuclides, which is a tiny bit of radioactive material. Then, the doctor places a monitor on your stomach to track the progress of the radionuclides in order to determine how quickly it leaves your stomach. The test takes about three hours to complete.

GASTRIC EMPTYING BREATH TEST (GEBT)

Approved by the FDA in April of 2015, the Gastric Emptying Breath Test (GEBT) is a four-hour test that measures how quickly your stomach empties. After an overnight fast, you will eat a special meal that contains eggs, milk, wheat, and a blue-green algae called spirulina. Following the meal, the carbon dioxide in your breath is measured at various intervals to determine how quickly your stomach empties. The test is noninvasive and can be performed in your doctor's office.

Tips

Medical testing can be stressful, but it is necessary in order to obtain an accurate diagnosis. Consider the following tips:

- Ask your doctor about the least invasive options available to obtain accurate diagnosis and ask for those first.

- If you take anticoagulants, anti-inflammatory medication, or aspirin, tell your doctor and follow any specific instructions for staying off medications leading up to procedures.

- Closely follow the pre-procedure instructions regarding eating.

- If you have diabetes, talk to your doctor about how best to control your blood sugar and/or when to take your insulin as it relates to pre-procedure fasting.

- If the procedure requires sedation, have someone drive you to and from your appointment.

- If you are being referred for CT or MRI scanning, tell your doctor or radiologist if you are claustrophobic.

- If your doctor prescribes medications, talk with them about contraindications with other medications or supplements you are currently taking.

STORIES FROM THE FRONT LINE

In the following pages, patients share their stories and tips about living with gastroparesis.

Q&A with a Gastroparesis Veteran:
Amy Foore

Tell us about your gastroparesis. How long have you had it, and how has it affected your health or your lifestyle? Do you have any other dietary restrictions?

I have had gastroparesis since July 1999. I did have a symptom-free period from December of 1999 until March of 2004. Since 2004, my symptoms have been constant. In 2004, my health continued to decline, and I was unable to return to work. My last day of work was in September of 2004, though I spent more time in the hospital the previous six months than I spent at home or work.

I have undergone every medication and other treatments. I have a gastric neurostimulator, which is the thing that has helped most. I still take nausea medicines around the clock, but the neurostimulator has helped. I'm on my third one. They last on average about four years (for me) before needing to be replaced. I don't really have any dietary restrictions,

because most of the things I can tolerate aren't on the diabetic diet, so docs tell me to eat what I can. I now do carb counting to manage my insulin dosage.

What advice would you give to a new patient who is struggling to maintain a "normal" life filled with travel, social activities, career growth, and more?

Try to live your life as normally as possible, but take your body's cues and listen to them. Advocating for yourself is a key component, as is having a friend or family member who will advocate for you as well.

Imagine you have gone back in time, and you've just been told that you have gastroparesis. What words of wisdom would you share with the "young you"?

I would tell myself to live my life. Don't worry about what others think. Gather as much info as you can, put together a great medical team, and if your doctor doesn't seem helpful, search out one who will help you.

What do you tell people who say they're too busy for self-care? If you could prescribe three self-care activities for new patients with gastroparesis, what three activities would you prescribe?

- Take time for yourself. Stress makes symptoms worse, so make sure you have an activity you can enjoy doing to take your mind off things.

- Get as much rest as possible.

- Eat as healthy as you can.

What do you do when you experience a flare-up?

- I drink as much fluid as possible. I drink slushies when I'm at my worst.

- I eat pasta in beef broth if I'm having a very bad day.

- I also increase my anti-nausea meds to maximum dosages.

If these approaches do not work, I end up in the hospital with tube feedings.

People who don't have gastroparesis will never understand…

Why we are so sick; to them, we "look fine." The truth is, I can do only small activities at a time. Even something like taking a shower requires preparation and a nap afterwards. If I have a doctor's appointment and need to stop to pick up prescriptions, I spend the next day in bed. No one understands.

What is the silver lining in having gastroparesis?

All the friends I have made, all over the USA, as well as other countries. If I didn't have gastroparesis, I never would've come into contact with these people. Thankfully, the Internet age allows us to talk to others who understand what we go through, which can be incredibly affirming and calming.

Q&A with a Gastroparesis Veteran:
Stephanie Hyatt

Tell us about your gastroparesis. How long have you had it, and how has it affected your health or your lifestyle? Do you have any other dietary restrictions?

I've had gastroparesis since I was 3 years old and I'm now 27. I never got properly diagnosed until I was 19. After a gastric emptying study, it was shown that it took eight hours for half my food to empty from my stomach. The normal time is around two hours.

My gastroparesis is secondary to something called pyloric stenosis. My pyloric sphincter was open enough to let food through, but the size of an opening is like an olive. Eventually my stomach gave up working, and, as one of my surgeons described, my stomach looked floppy, distended, and nonfunctional.

I have thrown up since I was 3. I threw up after class parties, on field trips, my first communion, during a final in college. You name a place, and I've thrown up there. I've thrown up even while driving my car more times than I can count. It's smart to have a bucket in your car!

I have spent my life at the ER getting fluids and IV medications. I've tried every medication multiple times (Reglan, erythromycin, and domperidone) for motility, had various procedures multiple times (Botox in the pyloric sphincter), and had a pyloromyotomy surgery. Unfortunately for me, my pyloric sphincter, along with causing gastroparesis, had caused scar tissue in my entire upper abdomen.

When I was 23, a year out of college, I became the sickest I had ever been. I couldn't keep any fluids or food down. This lasted for over a month and I realized something was very wrong. Every door at work seemed to become heavier and heavier until after a month, my body couldn't even move to get from the couch to my bedroom upstairs. My amazing gastroenterologist, who is my role model and hero, admitted me to the hospital. That became the scariest and most unknown summer. I had surgery that fall called a Billroth II, which removed part of my stomach, my pyloric sphincter, part of my duodenum, and my gallbladder, and rerouted my stomach to empty vertically into my jejunum. Essentially my stomach didn't have to work. I could eat!

I had hoped that this was a "cure," but unfortunately it wasn't. I have developed some other health issues in the last few years. I'm still nauseous most days, throw up a lot, don't absorb certain nutrients, have pain, etc. My diet is VERY limited. I'm just thankful that the surgery allowed me to avoid needing a feeding tube and that I can eat. You have to count the small blessings and victories in life!

Gastroparesis has changed my life in more ways than I can even count. I'm crying just writing this. The physical aspects are brutal. I can't think of anything worse than being nauseated. It's debilitating. I'll have good periods and bad periods. Every single day is unknown. My gastroenterologist describes it as a roller coaster.

I also think of it as being deep underwater trying to swim up. When I'm feeling good, I am getting close to the surface. But then, I end up being pushed back down. It's a constant physical struggle.

There are other aspects besides the physical that affect me. It affects every single part of my life. I can't always work a full-time or even part-time job. I have had to put my dreams on hold for years, and sometimes it feels like I'll never get to accomplish them. I feel like a failure some days. My parents support me financially at this point. It's embarrassing to me that I'm in my late 20s, and I can't support myself at all.

I'm scared of being in a relationship, because I don't want to be a burden to anyone else. I feel like a burden to my parents, which I know I'm not. I know they love me more than anything. I've lost friends because I've had to cancel so many times. If they had the stomach flu, would they be willing to go out somewhere? People just don't understand.

These are all completely normal feelings. I've had 24 years to deal and come to terms with this illness. I have to remind myself that I didn't choose this, so all I can do is make the best of the situation. I try to smile and laugh as much as possible. I'm lucky I have a positive "glass is half full" perspective on life. If I didn't, I don't know if I would ever get out of bed.

I do have occasional days where I just break down and cry. Then, other days I feel hopeful. When I feel good, I make the most of it because I might spend the next day lying by the toilet.

Everything is about balance in my life. If I push myself too hard, I'll get sick, but on the other hand I can't just lie in bed forever and never do anything. Gastroparesis has made me so much more thankful for the tiniest things. I have a gratitude journal and even on my worst days, I can find 10 things to be thankful for, such as nausea medicine, heating pads, having somewhere to live, etc. The gratitude journal has helped me tremendously.

I'm thankful that I graduated college with my bachelor's degree in biomedical sciences. I wanted to go to medical school, but by my senior year of college, I knew my body couldn't physically handle that, so that dream went out the door. I want to go to physician's assistant school now, but my body hasn't been strong enough for that yet. I know that when I become a PA, I will be able to understand patients from my experiences and empathize with them.

My diet has a lot of nos. No or very low fiber, no salads or raw vegetables unless I chew them until they're liquid, no corn or broccoli, no sugar especially chocolate, and I have to eat foods with a lot of salt. The high salt and low fiber are the opposite of the "healthy" American diet, which I find funny. I eat a lot of carbohydrates. I'll eat cooked vegetables or put greens in a smoothie, which I've found is the best way to not mess up my GI tract. I give myself vitamin B_{12} shots and get iron infusions. I eat very small portions six times a day. When I was younger, before an official diagnosis, I never understood how anyone could eat a whole plate of food. I thought that when someone was full that meant they were nauseated, since that's how I felt.

What advice would you give to a new patient who is struggling to maintain a "normal" life filled with travel, social activities, career growth, and more?

- Advocate for yourself! That is the most important piece of advice. If you feel off, but a doctor is dismissing you, listen to your intuition. You know your body more than anyone else.

- Explain to your friends exactly what is going on. The best way to describe gastroparesis is that it feels like having the stomach flu 24/7. You will find out who your true friends are. It is absolutely heartbreaking when friends leave, but that just means they were never true friends in the first place. Explain that you may have to cancel and your life is unpredictable. The friends who are still in my life now are incredible and will come over if I don't feel well enough to go out, or just bring me Gatorade.

- Social settings can be hard when you realize how many revolve around food. If you're out at a restaurant, don't be scared to ask for a smaller portion or what the ingredients are. If you're not able to eat anything, ask your friends to plan the social activity without including food, such as a walk, movies, shopping, pedicures, etc.

- As for work, be honest with your boss about what is going on. Honesty about the situation is so important. Obviously, no one can truly understand how miserable gastroparesis is. I had just started a new job a few years ago and ended up in the hospital for over a week. They were very understanding! My work colleagues at that job were wonderful and for my birthday brought me salty snacks instead of cake like we did for other birthdays. I found opening up to be so much more beneficial than hiding it all.

- Always keep a snack and drink (my choice is always G2 Gatorade!) in your purse or at work in the fridge.

Imagine you have gone back in time, and you've just been told that you have gastroparesis. What words of wisdom would you share with the "young you"?

The most important thing that I would tell the "young me" is that life won't go according to plan and to just live in the present moment. I was such a planner who had my entire life mapped out to a "T." I haven't given up on my dreams and goals, and I never will. I just now know that there isn't a specific timeline that has to be followed. Living in the present moment helps keep the calm in your life with a chronic illness.

I would also share with the "young me" to advocate for myself, never give up fighting, and to always have hope. My pediatrician always dismissed my parents and my concerns about my vomiting episodes. She said I just got the stomach flu a lot, or it was stress. Who gets the stomach flu every week? It's hard to not beat yourself up about not pushing harder and advocating back then. Hindsight is 20/20, though. Don't dwell on the past. Use your past mistakes as a learning tool for the future.

I would encourage myself that flare-ups don't last forever. Sometimes after vomiting for weeks straight, you just are so exhausted, and you wonder if the vomiting will ever end. It will get better! Not every day is going to be as bad as your worst day. Gastroparesis is quite the roller coaster. You will learn and accept your new "normal," and it won't be normal compared to people who are healthy. You can't compare your life to others. Everyone has his or her difficulties in life, and this just happens to be mine. A few times I've thought, "Why me? I'm such a good person. I don't deserve

this." But if I didn't have gastroparesis, I would have some other struggle in my life. I feel very blessed for what I do have.

At times you will feel sad and discouraged, and that's OK to feel that way. It's better expressing and accepting those emotions rather than dismissing and holding them in. If you need to cry for a few hours, do it! Just don't sit and wallow in your misery, because ultimately that will exacerbate the physical symptoms.

Last, but not least, I would tell myself: You are a lot stronger than you think you are!

What do you tell people who say they're too busy for self-care? If you could prescribe three self-care activities for new patients with gastroparesis, what three activities would you prescribe?

I think self-care is one of the most important aspects of controlling gastroparesis. Some of my self-care care prescriptions are just little things, but are crucial for preventing flare-ups. Obviously there will be times where you have a flare-up even if you do everything right.

Here's how I like to describe the cycle downward with no self-care:

Without enough sleep, your nausea will flare; if you don't have your medications (or whatever else you use for nausea) at that point, you start throwing up, which turns into cyclical vomiting, which means that you can't keep any fluids down, which turns into dehydration, and you will end up in the ER or admitted to the hospital. It can go in any order and will all end up the same. For example, dehydration can cause nausea and vomiting can cause no sleep. I call it the downward spiral.

Bring some type of hydration, preferably with electrolytes, everywhere you go. I bring my G2 Gatorade everywhere. I just drink baby sips all throughout the day so I can avoid dehydration. Dehydration equals ER and IV fluids.

Bring your medication (or whatever helps your nausea, pain, etc.) everywhere you go, as well. I have a pill container in my purse, and even if I'm going somewhere I can't bring a purse, let's say jet-skiing, for instance, I make sure to put my Phenergan and Zofran in a baggie. If you can stop the vomiting before it happens, then all will be calm.

Get an adequate amount of sleep specific to what your body needs to feel its best. You know your own body better than anyone and know how much sleep you need to be able to function properly. Even people without gastroparesis (or any chronic illness) feel awful without enough sleep. Magnify that by that by 100 or even 1,000 and that's how you'll feel with gastroparesis without enough sleep.

What are your go-to remedies when you experience a flare-up?

- Nausea medications (Phenergan, Zofran, and scopolamine patches)
- Sports drinks (like Gatorade)
- Chicken broth
- Saltines
- Heating pad/ice

People who don't have gastroparesis will never understand . . .

How it is to feel nauseated all the time. And that you never get used to vomiting.

What is the silver lining in having gastroparesis?

You appreciate life so much more and are grateful for the little things.

Q&A with a Gastroparesis Veteran:
Kathryn

Tell us about your gastroparesis. How long have you had it, and how has it affected your health or your lifestyle? Do you have any other dietary restrictions?

I was diagnosed with idiopathic gastroparesis on November 17, 2014. I'm 62 years old and nondiabetic. I am 100 percent disabled; I suffered a traumatic brain injury in 1997 from a car accident. As a result of that car accident, I have had problems with falling. My gastroparesis was caused by being given too much morphine by medical personnel after I fell.

When I was first diagnosed, I didn't know what gastroparesis was. I worked in the medical field for more than 25 years. One week after I was diagnosed, I spent hours on the Internet learning about gastroparesis. I began to keep a daily journal of all foods, liquids, medications, and activities. It has helped me a lot.

I found a diet plan on the Internet for people with gastroparesis. My GI doctor told me to eat no fat, no oils, no fiber, no raw fruits or skin, and no meat, and eat only vegetables that were cooked to mush! I had to learn by myself over time what I could or couldn't eat by trial and error. Most doctors know very little about gastroparesis.

I suffer from malnutrition and malabsorption of vital nutrients due to the severe dietary restrictions of gastroparesis.

I can now tolerate only custards, soy-based ice cream, and soy-based protein mix; no coffee, milk, or carbonated drinks; a few bites of chicken with no skin or fat; and occasionally some pretzels. I drink plain Gatorade, herbal tea, and clear nutritional drinks. I take potassium, magnesium, and occasionally Zofran for nausea and vomiting. I also often take stool softeners and laxatives.

What advice would you give to a new patient who is struggling to maintain a "normal" life filled with travel, social activities, career growth, and more?

When you are diagnosed with gastroparesis you MUST become your own advocate. You have to learn everything you can about gastroparesis, medications, and diet.

Imagine you have gone back in time, and you've just been told that you have gastroparesis. What words of wisdom would you share with the "young you"?

Learn all you can about this disease. Find another doctor if you are not being treated with respect. Join support groups on Facebook and Yahoo. Take it easy on yourself and listen to your body. Most important (it has really helped me!) keep a daily journal! Write down all foods and liquids and any reactions, all medications, daily activities, and any changes in your symptoms. I always take my journal with me to all doctor appointments!

What do you tell people who say they're too busy for self-care? If you could prescribe three self-care activities for new patients with gastroparesis, what three activities would you prescribe?

- Learn what foods and liquids your stomach can tolerate.
- Rest when you can.
- Look for peace and joy in every day.

What are your go-to remedies when you experience a flare-up?

- Clear liquids
- Rest
- Talking with supportive friends
- Letting my doctor know my symptoms
- When I get diarrhea I use a product called DripDrop. It has balanced electrolytes and is much better than sports drinks or Pedialyte. It is available at Walgreens.

People who don't have gastroparesis will never understand…

It is true that only another person with this illness can understand what it is like. That is why support groups are so important!

What is the silver lining in having gastroparesis?

I have met some amazing, loving, supportive friends who have gastroparesis. I found out who my "real" friends are.

Q&A with a Gastroparesis Veteran:
Nikki Weber

Tell us about your gastroparesis. How long have you had it, and how has it affected your health or your lifestyle? Do you have any other dietary restrictions?

On February 14, 2015, I hit five years of my journey. Five years ago, I was home visiting my parents and went on a drive with my dad to take some photographs, when all of a sudden I got extremely nauseated, became very dizzy and pale, and felt as though flu-like symptoms just came over me. We went home, and I had no appetite for the rest of the night.

The next morning, I woke up feeling the same way—extremely nauseated, heartburn, pain, fatigue, bloating, and satiated when I tried to eat anything. I started dropping weight, and within a week I ended up in the ER with pain and dehydration. Soon after, I went to see a primary doctor, but he told me I just needed to work out less, and I probably sprained a stomach muscle. I knew that wasn't the reason, as I already knew my body. I just kept saying, "I think I'm allergic to food."

Next, I made an appointment with a local gastroenterologist (GI). He ran some tests—gallbladder scans, scopes, and barium studies—but didn't know what to do, so I went back home to Maryland and saw another GI, who ran a smart pill test and an emptying study. That's when I heard the word "gastroparesis" for the first time. That doctor, though, was not willing to pick up my case. He said I needed to see a specialist at Temple University in Philadelphia.

At this point, months into my pain, I was still losing weight and could barely eat (though I figured out I could tolerate liquids better than solids and did better eating dairy-free). I slept all the time, kept to myself, and stopped going out with my friends. Each day, I pushed to get through work and crashed immediately once I got home. I made my appointment with Temple and had a two-day emptying study test. They confirmed I had gastroparesis.

Over the next three years, we tried tons of medicines and Botox twice to the pyloric nerve. The doctor spoke to me about the neurostimulator; however, my intestines had started to slow along with my stomach, so that no longer became a good option for me. My weight stayed above 95 pounds and my blood work was all right (minus my iron), but my pain and bloating worsened. My self-confidence and self-esteem withered away as my waist size would go from a size 0 to 10 in one day, and from other physical changes caused by my lack of nutrients, as well as side effects from the medication. My former "carpe diem" approach to life became filled with anxiety and hopelessness. Three years into my journey and my life had completely changed. I stopped traveling, working out, hiking, and camping. Everything I loved seemed impossible now. I needed a new hope as I had given up.

Then one evening, I got a phone call from my dad.

"Nikki," he said, "I went to a conference this week and I tracked down a new GI doctor. Can we give him a call?"

My mind raced. "Do we give it a try?!"

I felt like there was a light at the end of my tunnel, and I had a new hope, so we made an appointment at Johns Hopkins. When I first met with my new doctor, I was super nervous. He ordered blood work and tons of new tests. Mostly, though, I remember him saying, "It's going to be a really hard year, Nikki, but we're going to get you to feel better. Are you ready?"

"I'm ready."

So, the next few months I had another gastric emptying test—solids and liquids separate—plus tests to see how I swallow and how my intestines work (just to name a few!). At this point, my entire digestive track had dysmotility. When I heard this, I did not know what to think. I was scared and, again, I was losing hope. My friends and family, though, reminded me daily about how strong and amazing I was, which kept me going. During my next appointment, I learned about a Mayo Clinic blood test that came back with a new diagnosis. My doctor threw out the new words "autoimmune gastrointestinal dysmotility (AGID) P/Q." I was confused. I was not prepared for a new diagnosis or for change. He told me I needed to see a neurologist to start me on IVIG to help fight the antibodies that have shut down my digestive track.

While doctors commonly prescribed IVIG, it was experimental for AGID, so the fight to get IVIG with the insurance company began. Months later, my mom called me in tears. I immediately assumed something was wrong and started crying. All I heard was, "You're approved!"

In April 2014, I had my first five-day infusion with my home nurse. By the second day, I could not handle the headaches and neck pain. I was nauseated and sensitive to light. I wound up in the hospital where we finished the dosage, and then I was released. A few hours later, I got

admitted at Johns Hopkins, where I got a lumbar puncture to show I had aseptic meningitis. After ten days, I went home.

With doctor's clearance, we continued with my IVIG, but I kept having small reactions and either passed out or the nurse struggled to find veins for the IV. A few months went by, and I could see small differences, but had another bout of aseptic meningitis and got admitted to the hospital for another 11 days.

I was frustrated. What I thought could help me, I could not handle. My neurologist met with my parents and me. Together, we made a few changes to the treatment and decided to continue it. Over the next months, we played around to find what would work best for me. We slowed down the rate of the IV drip, cut the dosage, increased the number of treatments, changed the brand, added more fluids during the treatment, and added fluids in the off weeks. Also, during this time I got a porta-cath to make the infusion treatments easier.

In mid-December, I had a full five-day gastric emptying test at Johns Hopkins and for the first time in five years, it showed small improvements in everything but my large intestine (which still had dysmotility). I now get my treatment every two weeks for two days. The treatments are not easy, but my nurse is one of the best and my friends keep me company or help me by taking care of my dog.

After four and a half years, I brought soft foods (in very, very small quantities) back into my diet. Some weeks I handle these foods better than others, but overall I have made small victories in the past five years. This journey is far from over as I still have many hard days, but now have some good days, too.

And, while my journey has been hard, the most amazing and strongest people I know have come alive during these past five years to help me be brave and remind me of who I really am.

What advice would you give to a new patient who is is struggling to maintain a "normal" life filled with travel, social activities, career growth, and more?

I am a young professional who tries to have a normal life; however, every weekend I have IVIG treatments or receive fluids at my local infusion center. When I do have free time before and after work or after my infusions, I love to spend my time with my friends and my pooch.

I have learned that it's best if I suggest places for my friends and me, since I can pick places that fit my needs, too. For example, rather than go to a restaurant and watch my friends eat, I will suggest a self-serve frozen yogurt place that has sorbet options, or a Starbucks where I can sip on a drink and easily take the rest of it to go. I have also worked to make my apartment the "hang out" spot with my friends. This works great on days when I am exhausted, because I can invite people over for a movie, but still stay in my pajamas and have all my comforts of home (like my medicine and heating pad!). Luckily, my friends understand, and they will come over, bring their own dinners, and picnic on the floor as we watch a movie.

I also try to make plans at least once over the weekend, so I do not feel like I am stuck in my apartment. Even if I am tired and not feeling great, I will walk around Target and push a shopping cart (for the extra support). I have also picked up new interests, such as sewing and refurbishing furniture. I can do these projects right in my apartment and can work on them as I have the energy.

Most important for me, I try to lead a normal life by going to work each day. I love my job. It gets me up in the morning and allows me to focus on that rather than my bloated stomach or the pain under my ribs. Every day I have had gastroparesis, I have worked to find my new normal. I am still working on it, but getting a dog this past year, having a great group of friends, expanding my hobbies, and going to a job I love have all helped in my journey.

Imagine you have gone back in time, and you've just been told that you have gastroparesis. What words of wisdom would you share with the "young you"?

- Stay positive and don't shut people out.
- None of this was your fault.
- You are brave. Be brave.
- Share your story and spread awareness.

What do you tell people who say they're too busy for self-care? If you could prescribe three self-care activities for new patients with gastroparesis, what three activities would you prescribe?

It is important and healthy to find time to care for yourself—it's how you push through each day of gastroparesis. Three activities I recommend are:

- Volunteer at a local animal shelter; just playing with the animals is therapeutic. (Plus, the animals need your support and love, as well!)
- Break out arts and craft projects. I love crafts! I create and repurpose old furniture to help take my mind off not feeling well.

- I rescued a puppy! This took me over five years of finding my new "normal" before I was ready to adopt a dog, but he was worth the wait. It is definitely a "who rescued who?" situation. He gets me out walking daily, lays by my side when I'm not feeling well, gives me a lot to talk about (other than my illness), and I am constantly getting love. Even on days I feel my worst, my dog makes me so happy.

What are your go-to remedies when you experience a flare-up?

- My heating pad
- Netflix

People who don't have gastroparesis will never understand…

- How hard it is to sit at a table watching other people eat when you cannot
- How much energy it takes to do simple tasks like taking a shower or getting dressed

What is the silver lining in having gastroparesis?

- My support system
- The other local gastroparesis friends I made in my hometown

Another positive was my sister's help in showing me how to share my story with friends and family. We created an awareness day to help make my anniversary date something positive and spread awareness. We called it Wear Green for Gastroparesis on Feb. 14.

Q&A with a Gastroparesis Veteran:
Ashley Jenkins

Tell us about your gastroparesis. How long have you had it, and how has it affected your health or your lifestyle? Do you have any other dietary restrictions?

I started experiencing gastroparesis symptoms in October 2009, but was not diagnosed until January 2011. Getting gastroparesis changed everything about me. I used to be the family garbage disposal, eating my meal and then the remainder of my sister's when she was full. The constant nausea and fullness have drastically changed that, but finding ways to deal with my nausea have really been helpful. I am allergic to tree nuts, oats, and gluten, and I cannot tolerate much fat due to my gallbladder being removed.

What advice would you give to a new patient who is struggling to maintain a "normal" life filled with travel, social activities, career growth, and more?

As a college student, the best way to have a "normal" life is to find friends who are understanding and care about you. That way, when you are having a bad day, week, or month, there are people who are willing to support you and not just ignore you. Having a base of support is a huge part of why I've managed to do so well.

When I first got to school I was open and honest about my illness. It wasn't all I talked about, but I answered any and all questions I was asked. Explaining it to people helped me feel accepted and helped them understand me better.

Another piece of advice is to take advantage of good days, but don't go overboard. Be active in organizations and groups, but realize that things happen and you can't always do what others do. Every time I am asked to volunteer for an organization, I explain my situation and tell them I'll plan to be there but could have to stay home at the last minute. Once I realized that I had to put my health first (getting enough sleep to have the energy for class and studying), I began to do very well.

Finally, each semester I go to my professors and explain gastroparesis and what it means for me. It makes them far more understanding when things come up.

Basically I am saying that being clear and open about your life and health is quite beneficial to life as college student.

Imagine you have gone back in time, and you've just been told that you have gastroparesis. What words of wisdom would you share with the "young you"?

Push yourself as far as you can with eating; I know you feel awful, but a PICC line and feeding tube is worse. Also, when the doctor tells you about the gastric pacemaker, don't be scared. It's not a cure, but it helps more than you'd ever think.

What do you tell people who say they're too busy for self-care? If you could prescribe three self-care activities for new patients with gastroparesis, what three activities would you prescribe?

If you don't take care of your body, it won't take care of you. End of story.

One self-care tip is to get enough sleep. I know it's hard sometimes, but exhaustion just makes gastroparesis worse, it catches up quick. Another self-care tip is to join support groups. Facebook has a ton of groups. I even created a group to share GP-friendly recipes (see page 193). These groups not only build friendships; they can teach you a lot and help you brainstorm more ways to help yourself. Finally, as annoying as it can be, when you first discover you have Gastroparesis it is really helpful to keep a food journal and figure out which foods work well and which don't. No one is exactly the same; our bodies react differently so you have to experiment (preferably on a day when you don't have anything to do for a while in case of flare-ups).

What are your go-to remedies when you experience a flare-up?

- Rest
- A softer diet
- Sea Bands (a bracelet that uses acupressure for nausea)

People who don't have gastroparesis will never understand …

- The nonstop nausea that comes with it
- The need to pace yourself and save energy

What is the silver lining in having gastroparesis?

- You make friends who truly understand and are always there for you

Please see Ashley's Carob Pudding recipe on page 169.

APPENDIX C

MEASUREMENTS AND CONVERSION TABLES

Volume Equivalents (Liquid)

US STANDARD	US STANDARD (ounces)	METRIC (approximate)
2 tablespoons	1 fl. oz.	30 mL
¼ cup	2 fl. oz.	60 mL
½ cup	4 fl. oz.	120 mL
1 cup	8 fl. oz.	240 mL
1½ cups	12 fl. oz.	355 mL
2 cups or 1 pint	16 fl. oz.	475 mL
4 cups or 1 quart	32 fl. oz.	1 L
1 gallon	128 fl. oz.	4 L

Weight Equivalents

US STANDARD	METRIC (approximate)
½ ounce	15 g
1 ounce	30 g
2 ounces	60 g
4 ounces	115 g
8 ounces	225 g
12 ounces	340 g
16 ounces or 1 pound	455 g

Volume Equivalents (Dry)

US STANDARD	METRIC (approximate)
⅛ teaspoon	0.5 mL
¼ teaspoon	1 mL
½ teaspoon	2 mL
¾ teaspoon	4 mL
1 teaspoon	5 mL
1 tablespoon	15 mL
¼ cup	59 mL
⅓ cup	79 mL
½ cup	118 mL
⅔ cup	156 mL
¾ cup	177 mL
1 cup	235 mL
2 cups or 1 pint	475 mL
3 cups	700 mL
4 cups or 1 quart	1 L
½ gallon	2 L
1 gallon	4 L

Oven Temperatures

FAHRENHEIT (F)	CELSIUS (C) (approximate)
250°	120°
300°	150°
325°	165°
350°	180°
375°	190°
400°	200°
425°	220°
450°	230°

THE DIRTY DOZEN AND THE CLEAN FIFTEEN

2015	
DIRTY DOZEN	**CLEAN FIFTEEN**
Apples	Asparagus
Celery	Avocados
Cherry tomatoes	Cabbage
Cucumbers	Cantaloupe
Grapes	Cauliflower
Nectarines	Eggplant
Peaches	Grapefruit
Potatoes	Kiwis
Snap peas	Mangos
Spinach	Onions
Strawberries	Papayas
Sweet bell peppers	Pineapples
	Sweet corn
In addition to the Dirty Dozen, the EWG added two vegetables contaminated with highly toxic organo-phosphate insecticides:	Sweet peas (frozen)
	Sweet potatoes
Hot peppers	
Kale/Collard greens	

A nonprofit and environmental watchdog organization called Environmental Working Group (EWG) looks at data supplied by the US Department of Agriculture (USDA) and the Food and Drug Administration (FDA) about pesticide residues and compiles a list each year of the best and worst pesticide loads found in commercial crops. You can use these lists to decide which fruits and vegetables to buy organic to minimize your exposure to pesticides and which produce is considered safe enough to skip the organics. This does not mean they are pesticide-free, though, so wash these fruits and vegetables thoroughly.

These lists change every year, so make sure you look up the most recent before you fill your shopping cart. You'll find the most recent lists as well as a guide to pesticides in produce at EWG.org/FoodNews.

REFERENCES

Abell, T. L, R. K. Bernstein, T. Cutts, G. Farrugia, J. Forster, W. L. Hasler, R. W. McCallum, K. W. Olden, H. P. Parkman, C. R. Parrish, P. J. Pasricha, C. M. Prather, E. E. Soffer, R. Twillman, and A. I. Vinik. "Treatment of Gastroparesis: A Multidisciplinary Clinical." *Neurogastroenterology and Motility* 18 (April 2006): 263–83. doi: 10.1111/j.1365-2982.2006.00760.x.

Abrahamsson, Hasse. "Treatment Options for Patients with Severe Gastroparesis." Gut. 56.6 (2007): 877–83. Accessed September 18, 2015. www.ncbi.nlm.nih.gov/pmc/articles /PMC1954884/.

American College of Gastroenterology. "Gastroparesis." 2012. Accessed August 17, 2015. patients.gi.org/topics/gastroparesis/.

American Diabetes Association. "Gastroparesis." Accessed September 18, 2015. www.diabetes.org/living-with-diabetes /complications/gastroparesis.html ?referrer=https://www.google.com/.

Arizona Digestive Health. "Gastroparesis Diet." August 17, 2015. www.arizonadigestivehealth.com /gastroparesis-diet/.

Bharucha, Adil E. "Epidemiology and Natural History of Gastroparesis." *Gastroenterology Clinics of North America* 44, no. 1 (March 2015): 9–19.

Camilleri, Michael, Henry P. Parkman, Mehnaz A. Shafi, Thomas L. Abell, and Lauren Gerson. "Clinical Guideline: Management of Gastroparesis." *American Journal of Gastroenterology* 108 (January 2013): 18–37. doi:10.1038 /ajg.2012373.

Center Watch. "Gastroparesis Clinical Trials." Accessed September 18, 2015. www.centerwatch.com/clinical-trials/listings /condition/72/gastroparesis.

Craggs-Dino, Lillian. "Medical Nutrition Therapy for Gastroparesis." The Cleveland Clinic. *Bariatric Nursing and Surgical Patient Care* 2, no. 2 (2007): 101–08. Accessed August 17, 2015. my.clevelandclinic.org/ccf/media /files/Florida/Nutriton_Gastroparesis _Manual_0509.pdf.

Doran, S., K. L. Jones, J. M. Andrews, and M. Horowitz. "Effects of Meal Volume and Posture on Gastric Emptying of Solids and Appetite." *American Journal of Physiology—Regulatory, Integrative, and Comparative Physiology* 275, no. 5 (November 1998): 1712–18.

Every Body Walk! "How does Exercise Reduce Stress?" Accessed September 18, 2015. www.everybodywalk.org/how-does-exercise-reduce-stress/.

Gentilcore, Diana, Reawika Chaikomin, Karen L. Jones, Antonietta Russo, Christine Feinle-Bisset, Judith M. Wishart, Christopher K. Rayner, and Michael Horowitz. "Effects of Fat on Gastric Emptying of and the Glycemic, Insulin, and Incretin Responses to a Carbohydrate Meal in Type 2 Diabetes." *Journal of Clinical Endocrinology & Metabolism* 91, no. 6 (March 2006): 2062–67.

Gonlachanvit, Sutep, Henry P. Parkman, William D. Chey, and Keith J. Goodman. "Effect of Meal Size and Test Duration on Gastric Emptying and Gastric Myoelectrical Activity as Determined with Simultaneous [13C]Octonoate Breath Test and Electrogastrography in Normal Subjects Using a Muffin Meal" *Digestive Diseases and Sciences* 46, no. 12 (December 2001): 2643–50. Accessed August 17, 2015. www.ncbi.nlm.nih.gov/pubmed/11768254.

G-PACT. "Gastroparesis Diet Guidelines." Accessed August 17, 2015. www.g-pact.org/gastroparesis/diet-guidelines.

Hasler, William L. "Gastroparesis—Current Concepts and Considerations." *Medscape Journal of Medicine 10*, no. 1 (January 2008): 16. Accessed September 18, 2015. www.ncbi.nlm.nih.gov/pmc/articles/PMC2258461/.

Health.com. "7 Daily Habits That Can Halt Heartburn." Accessed August 17, 2015. www.health.com/health/gallery/0,,20307299,00.html.

International Foundation for Functional Gastrointestinal Distorders. "Basic Dietary Guidelines for Gastroparesis." Accessed August 17, 2015. www.aboutgastroparesis.org/treatments/diet/basic-guidelines.

International Foundation for Functional Gastrointestinal Distorders. "Complementary and Alternative Medicine to Treat Gastroparesis." Accessed August 17, 2015. www.aboutgastroparesis.org/treatments/complementary.

International Foundation for Functional Gastrointestinal Disorders. "Diagnosis and Tests for Gastroparesis." Accessed August 17, 2015. www.aboutgastroparesis.org/signs-symptoms/diagnosis.

International Foundation for Functional Gastrointestinal Disorders. "Upper GI Endoscopy: What to Expect." Accessed August 17, 2015. www.iffgd.org/site/manage-your-health/tests-diagnosis/upper-endoscopy.

Jackson/Siegelbaum Gastroenterology. "Gastroparesis Diet for Delayed Stomach Emptying." Accessed August 17, 2015. gicare.com/diets/gastroparesis-diet/

Johns Hopkins Medical Center. "Conditions We Treat: Gastroparesis." 2012. Accessed August 17, 2015. www.hopkinsmedicine.org/gastroenterology_hepatology/diseases_conditions/esophageal_stomach/gastroparesis.html.

Lowes, Robert. "FDA Approves Gastroparesis Test for Any Clinical Setting." Medscape Multispecialty. April 06, 2015. Accessed September 18, 2015. www.medscape.com/viewarticle/842724.

Mayo Clinic. "Bezoars: What Foods Can Cause This Digestive Problem?" Accessed August 17, 2015. www.mayoclinic.org/diseases -conditions/gastroparesis/expert-answers /bezoars/faq-20058050.

Mayo Clinic. "Gastroparesis." Alternative Medicine. Accessed August 17, 2015. www.mayoclinic.org/diseases-conditions /gastroparesis/basics/alternative-medicine /con-20023971.

Mayo Clinic. "Gastroparesis." Accessed August 17, 2015. www.mayoclinic.org/diseases -conditions/gastroparesis/basics/definition /con-20023971.

MUSC Health Digestive Disease Center. "Gastro- paresis." Accessed September 18, 2015. www.ddc.musc.edu/public/symptomsDiseases /diseases/stomach/gastroparesis.html.

National Institutes of Diabetes and Digestive and Kidney Diseases. "Gastroparesis." Accessed August 17, 2015. www.niddk.nih.gov/health -information/health-topics/digestive-diseases /gastroparesis/Pages/facts.aspx.

National Institutes of Diabetes and Digestive and Kidney Diseases. "Upper GI Series." Accessed August 17, 2015. www.niddk.nih.gov /health-information/health-topics/diagnostic -tests/upper-gi-series/Pages/diagnostic-test .aspx.

National Organization for Rare Disorders. "Gastroparesis." Accessed September 18, 2015. www.rarediseases.org/rare-diseases /gastroparesis/.

Parkman, Henry P., Michael Camilleri, Gianrico Farrugia, Richard W. McCallum, Adil E. Bharucha, Emeran A. Mayer, Jan F. Tack, Robin Spiller, Michael Horowitz, Aaron I. Vinik, James J. Galligan, P. Jay Pasricha, Braden Kuo, Lawrence A. Szarka, Luca Marciani, Karen Jones, Carol Rees Parrish, Paola Sandroni, Thomas Abell, Tamas Ordog, William Hasler, Kenneth L. Koch, Kenton Sanders, Nancy J. Norton, and Frank Hamilton. "Gastroparesis and Functional Dyspepsia: Excerpts from the AGA/ANMS Meeting." *Neurogastroenterology and Motility* 22, no. 2 (February 2010): 113–33. doi: 10.1111/j.1365-2982.2009.01434.x.

Parkman, Henry P., Ronnie Fass, and Amy E. Foxx-Orenstein. "Treatment of Patients With Diabetic Gastroparesis." *Gastroenterology & Hepatology* 6, Suppl. 9. (June 2010): 1–16. Accessed August 17, 2015. www.ncbi.nlm.nih .gov/pmc/articles/PMC2920593/.

Parrish, Carol Rees, and Jeanne Keith-Ferris. "Diet Intervention for Gastroparesis." Uni- versity of Virginia Health Systems. Accessed August 17, 2015. uvahealth.com /services/digestive-health/images-and-docs /gastroparesis-diet.pdf.

PeaceHealth. "Gastric Emptying Scan." Accessed August 17, 2015. www.peacehealth .org/peace-harbor/services/imaging-services /nuclear-medicine/Pages/gastric-emptying -scan.aspx.

Reddymasu, Savio C., and Richard W. Mccal- lum. "Small Intestinal Bacterial Overgrowth in Gastroparesis : Are There Any Predictors?" *Journal of Clinical Gastroenterology* 44, no.1 (January 2010): e8–13.

Saltrelli, Crystal Zaborowski. "Eating for Gastroparesis: Guidelines, Tips & Recipes." *CreateSpace*. 2011. Accessed September 18, 2015. www.createspace.com/3610221.

Saltrelli, Crystal Zaborowski. *Living (Well!) with Gastroparesis: Answers, Advice, Tips & Recipes for a Healthier, Happier Life*. Rochester, NY: Sea Salt Publishing, 2011.

Sanders, Michael K. "Bezoars: From Mystical Charms to Medical and Nutritional Management." *Practical Gatroenterology* (January 2004), series ed. Carol Rees Parrish, *Nutrition Issues in Gastroenterology*, Series 13. Accessed September 18, 2015. www.medicine.virginia.edu/clinical/departments/medicine/divisions/digestive-health/nutrition-support-team/nutrition-articles/practicalgasto1.04.pdf.

Scarlata, Kate. "Gastroparesis and FODMAPs." *The Well-Balanced FODMAPer.* Accessed August 17, 2015. blog.katescarlata.com/2013/06/20/gastroparesis-and-fodmaps/.

Shafi, Mehnaz A., and P. Jay Pasricha. "Post-Surgical and Obstructive Gastroparesis." *Current Gastronenerology Reports* 9.4 (2007): 280–85. Accessed September 18, 2015. http://link.springer.com/article/10.1007%2Fs11894-007-0031-2.

UW Health. "Enterra Therapy Program: Surgery Details." Accessed September 18, 2015. www.uwhealth.org/surgery/enterra-therapy-program-surgery-details/11911.

UW Health. "Gatroparesis." Accessed September 18, 2015. www.uwhealth.org/health/topic/special/gastroparesis/tp22239spec.html.

WomensHealth.gov. "Autoimmune Diseases Fact Sheet." Accessed August 17, 2015. womenshealth.gov/publications/our-publications/fact-sheet/autoimmune-diseases.html.

RESOURCES

Advocacy and Information (Gastroparesis)

Digestive Health Alliance (DHA)
www.DHA.org

GastroparesisClinic.org
www.GastroParesisClinic.org

Gastroparesis Patient Association for Cures and Treatment (G-PACT)
www.G-PACT.org

G-PACT Restaurant Cards
www.g-pact.org/patient-resources

International Foundation for Functional Gastrointestinal Disorders (IFFGD)
www.iffgd.org/ and
www.AboutGastroparesis.org

National Institutes of Health (NIH) Gastroparesis Clinical Research Consortium
http://jhuccs1.us/gpcrc/open/patients /patientlinks.htm

Advocacy and Information (Associated Health Issues)

American Diabetes Association
www.diabetes.org

Digestive Disease National Coalition
www.ddnc.org

International Scleroderma Network
www.Sclero.org

National Institute of Diabetes, Digestive, and Kidney Diseases
www2.niddk.nih.gov

Oley Foundation (support for people on Feeding Tubes)
www.oley.org

Board Certified Physician Referrals

www.ncbde.org Academy of Nutrition and Dietetics (Registered Dietitian referral)
www.EatRight.org

American Board of Certification for Gastroenterology Nurses
www.abcgn.org

American Board of Internal Medicine (Internal medicine, gastroenterology, and endocrinology referral)
www.abim.org

American College of Gastroenterology
www.gi.org

National Certification Board for Diabetes Educators
www.ncbde.org

Gastroparesis Blogs

Adventures with Gastroparesis
www.AdventureswithGastroparesis.com

Journey with Gastroparesis by Stephanie Torres
MyGastroparesisJourney.Blogspot.com

Living with Gastroparesis by Crystal Saltrelli, CHC
www.LivingWithGastroparesis.com

Online Support Groups

AGMD GI Motility Disorders Support Community
www.inspire.com/groups/agmd-gi-motility

GNE with Gastroparesis Facebook
www.facebook.com/GreensNotEasy

G-PACT Facebook
www.facebook.com/GPACT

Recipe Swap for GP Patients Facebook Group
www.facebook.com/groups /434846263252165/

Yahoo International Gastroparesis Support Group
groups.yahoo.com/neo/groups /gastroparesis/info

RECIPE INDEX

INDEX

ACKNOWLEDGMENTS

Thanks to Amy Foore, Stephanie Hyatt, Kathryn, Nikki Weber, and Ashley Jenkins for sharing their stories here, as well as to Colleen Beener and Michael Smith of G-PACT for providing information and help with the book. I'm also grateful to my family and friends, who often adapt the way they eat in order to meet my special dietary needs, particularly my husband, Jim, and my son and stepson, Tanner and Kevin. Finally, I'd like to thank all the cooking mentors I've had over the years, who have taught me to be an inventive and adventurous cook.

ABOUT THE AUTHOR

KAREN FRAZIER is a nutrition and fitness expert who specializes in cookbooks for special need diets. Diagnosed in her early 40s with celiac disease and an acute dairy allergy, she understands how challenging it can be to eat a restricted diet that is both healthful and satisfying. Karen is the author of *The Hashimoto's Cookbook and Action Plan* and *Nutrition Facts*. She is also the Health editor of LoveToKnow.com.

CPSIA information can be obtained
at www.ICGtesting.com
Printed in the USA
BVHW022029040221
599249BV00009B/1919